Five-Min

SUNDAY SCH
ACTIVITIES

God Is Great

ROSEKIDZ®
An imprint of Rose Publishing, Inc.
Carson, CA
www.Rose-Publishing.com

Five-Minute Sunday School Activities

God Is Great

Karen Wingate

To Carl and Mary Anderson who taught me what it means to be a servant of Jesus Christ.

FIVE-MINUTE SUNDAY SCHOOL ACTIVITIES: GOD IS GREAT

ISBN 10: 1-58411-100-3
ISBN 13: 978-1-58411-100-9
RoseKidz® reorder# R38424
RELIGION / Christian Ministry / Children

RoseKidz®
An imprint of Rose Publishing, Inc.
17909 Adria Maru Lane
Carson, CA 90746
www.Rose-Publishing.com

Cover Illustrator: Chuck Galey
Interior Illustrator: Brie Spangler

Printed in China

Contents

Introduction

In a world where our children are bombarded with information and stimulation at seemingly every turn, it is increasingly important that we teach them why God is more worthy of our attention and devotion than anything else we know. When you teach these lessons from the Bible, your children will grasp God's role as Judge, King, and Savior, and will see that He is truly worthy of our worship. Children who learn to acknowledge God's greatness will have a firm foundation of faith in God for the rest of their lives.

Five-Minute Sunday School Activities is designed to give teachers a quick activity that teaches an important Bible truth. Teachers are often faced with a few extra minutes after the lesson is finished. There are also times when a teacher needs a few moments to get attendance and other important matters out of the way before the main lesson. Instead of wasting these minutes with non-learning play, provide a *Five-Minute Sunday School Activity*!

The activities in this book can also be used as entire lessons. Bible story references, teaching suggestions, and memory verses are included with each activity.

Extra Time suggestions are given for each activity. If you have more than five minutes, extend the lesson time with the **Extra Time** option.

Adam and Eve Leave the Garden

GENESIS 2:15-17, 3

✓MEMORY VERSE

But God did say, "You must not eat fruit from the tree that is in the middle of the garden, and you must not touch it or you will die."
~ Genesis 3:3

WHAT YOU NEED

- page 10, duplicated
- pencils
- crayons

BEFORE CLASS

Duplicate a pattern page for each child.

WHAT TO DO

1. Introduce the lesson by telling the story from Genesis 2:15-17 and Genesis 3. Ask, **What did God tell Adam and Eve not to do? How did Adam and Eve disobey God? What was their punishment for doing wrong?**
2. Distribute a pattern page to each child.
3. Read the memory verse together.
4. Have students connect the dots around the printed memory verse. Read the verse again together. Say, **God told Adam and Eve not to eat the fruit from the Tree of the Knowledge of Good and Evil. What are some rules that God has given to us?**

EXTRA TIME

Play a game of "Red Light, Green Light." Choose one child to stand at a finish line facing away from the rest of the group standing at a starting line. When the caller calls, "Green Light," the group walks forward. When the caller calls "Red Light," and turns around, he may move anyone he sees moving back to the starting line. The first person to touch the caller wins the game. Say, **If you see a red light, our laws say you must stop. God's rules must be obeyed too.**

Five Minute

Connect the dots surrounding the memory verse. How did Adam and Eve disobey God?

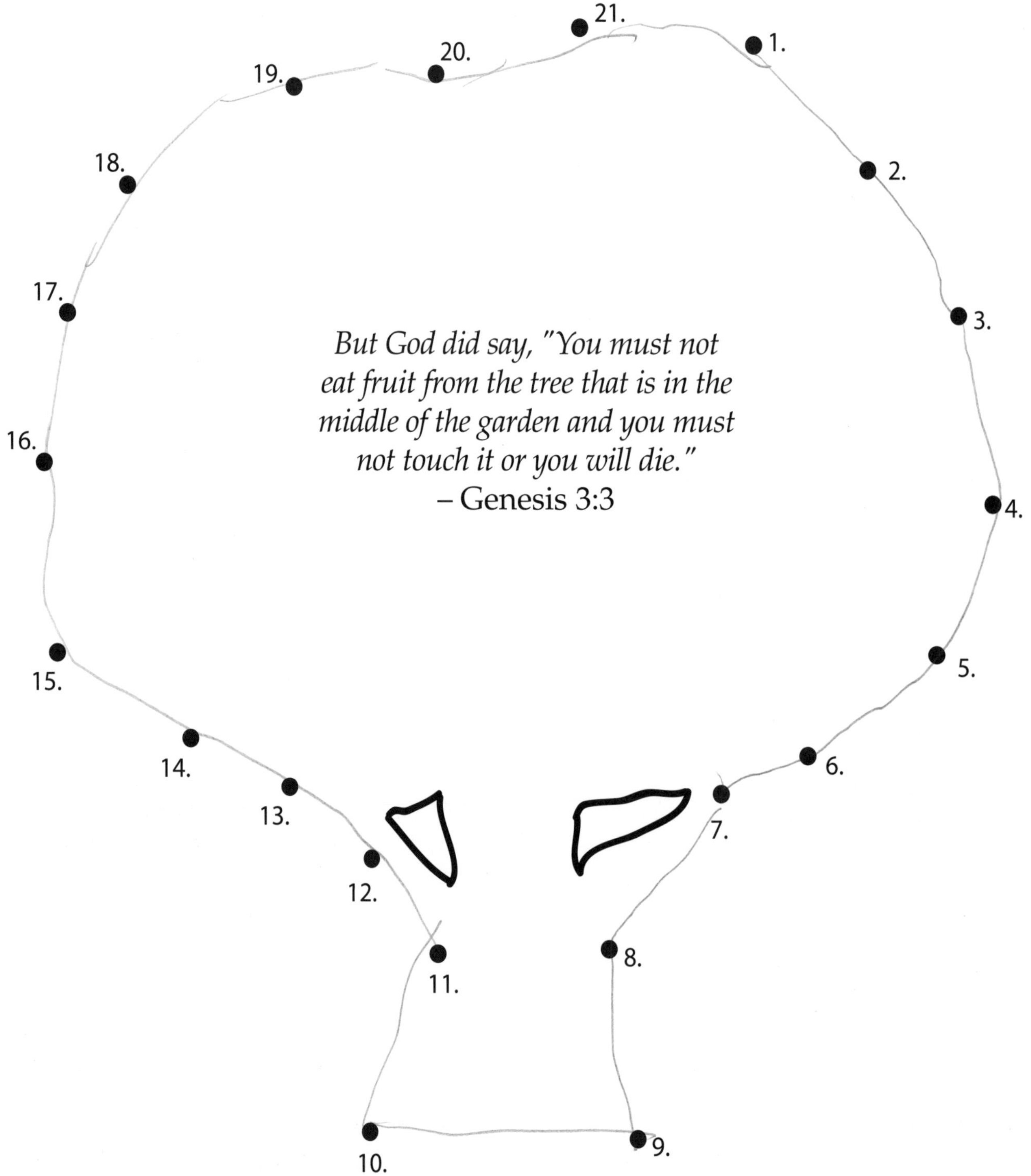

But God did say, "You must not eat fruit from the tree that is in the middle of the garden and you must not touch it or you will die."
– Genesis 3:3

God Gives Moses a Rule Book

EXODUS 19, 20:1-21, 24:12-18

✓MEMORY VERSE

We will do everything the Lord has said.
~ Exodus 19:8

WHAT YOU NEED

- page 12, duplicated
- pencils

BEFORE CLASS

Duplicate a pattern page for each child.

WHAT TO DO

1. Ask, **What are some rules you have at your house?** Introduce the lesson by telling the Bible story from Exodus 19, 20:1-21, 24:12-18. Say, **God gave Moses stone tablets that had ten very important rules written on them. Let's find out what those rules are.**
2. Distribute a pattern page to each child.
3. Ask students to unscramble the words in each sentence, only using the word box if they need help. When students finish, ask them to take turns reading the different sentences.
4. Read the memory verse. Say, **God's people listened to God. They made a promise to do everything God told them to do. It's important for us to obey God's rules too.**

EXTRA TIME

Have everyone stand in a circle. Ask for a volunteer to stand in the middle and to be the spinner. As the spinner slowly turns around, pointing at the group, the group chants, "Rules for me/Rules for you/Here's a rule that we will do." When they reach the end of the poem, the spinner stops. Whoever he or she is pointing at must say one of the Ten Commandments. If the child says a commandment correctly, he or she may become the spinner; if not, start the game again with the spinner from before.

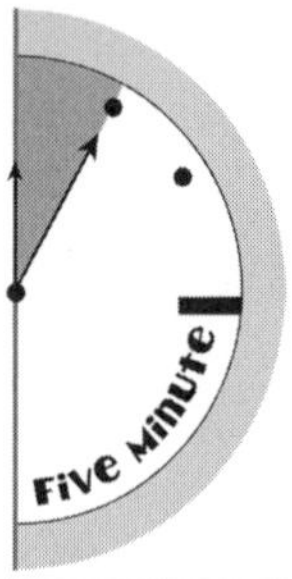

To find out God's Ten Rules, unscramble the words in each sentence using the available words.

murder **commit** **gods**

honor **Sabbath** **covet** **name**

steal **false** **idols**

1. You shall have no other ________ before me.
   dsog
2. You shall not have any ____________.
   sdloi
3. You shall not misuse the ______ of the Lord your God.
   aenm
4. Remember the _________ day by keeping it holy.
   bbaahSt
5. _________ your father and mother.
   rooHn
6. You shall not ___________.
   umrrde
7. You shall not ___________ adultery.
   otmcim
8. You shall not ___________.
   etasl
9. You shall not give ______________ testimony.
   leasf
10. You shall not _________ .
    tocve

We will do everything the Lord has said.
– Exodus 19:8

The solution is on page 95.

Joshua Challenges the People

JOSHUA 24:1-27

✓MEMORY VERSE

As for me and my household,
we will serve the Lord.
~ Joshua 24:15

As for me and my household, we will serve the Lord.
– Joshua 24:15

WHAT YOU NEED

- page 14, duplicated
- crayons

BEFORE CLASS

Duplicate a pattern page for each child. Draw a sample picture of your own family inside the house to show the children.

WHAT TO DO

1. Introduce the lesson by telling the Bible story from Joshua 24:1-27. Say, **Joshua wanted the people to choose whether or not they were going to serve God. We can't waver back and forth about whether we will follow God. Like Joshua, we need to make a choice. Are we going to follow God and obey His rules or not?**
2. Distribute a pattern page to each child.
3. Say the memory verse.
4. Have students draw a picture of themselves and the members of their family inside the house. Ask, **What are some ways your family can show they are serving God?** Suggest such ways as going to church, obeying God's rules all the time or praying together as a family.

EXTRA TIME

Expand your pattern page into a craft. Have your students cut out the house and glue it on a foam sheet. They can glue small craft sticks around the house for the frame of the house and seeds or small beans to the sides of the house, being careful not to cover up the memory verse or the family picture.

Five Minute

Draw a picture of your family inside the house. How can your family serve the Lord?

As for me and my household, we will serve the Lord.
– Joshua 24:15

Deborah and Barak

JUDGES 4

✓MEMORY VERSE

Then Deborah said to Barak, "Go! This is the day the Lord has given Sisera into your hands. Has not the Lord gone ahead of you?"
~ Judges 4:14

WHAT YOU NEED

- page 16, duplicated
- pencils
- crayons

BEFORE CLASS

Duplicate a pattern page for each child.

WHAT TO DO

1. Introduce the lesson by telling the story from Judges 4. Ask, **What job did God want Barak to do? How did Deborah help him? How did God help him?**
2. Distribute a pattern page to each child.
3. Read the memory verse together.
4. Point out the letters on the leaves of the palm tree. Ask students to unscramble the letters to find out what Barak needed. Ask students to write about a time when they needed courage. Say, **God promised Barak He would go ahead of him to help him. God goes ahead of us too. He is powerful and He wants to help us.**

EXTRA TIME

Have students turn their pages over and write a prayer to God, telling Him about a difficult situation they face and asking Him to go ahead of them. Be available to write prayers down for those who are beginning writers.

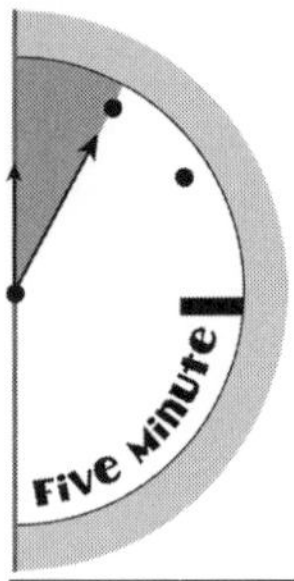

Find the letters in the tree and unscramble them to find what Barak needed in order to do what God asked him to do.

What did Barak needs? ___ ___ ___ ___ ___ ___ ___

When do you need this? ______________________________

____

____

____

Then Deborah said to Barak, "Go. This is the day the Lord has given Sisera into your hands. Has not the Lord gone ahead of you?"
– Judges 4:14

The solution is on page 95.

God Chooses Gideon

JUDGES 6:1-24, 36-40

✓MEMORY VERSE

The Lord turned to him and said, "Go in the strength you have and save Israel out of Midian's hand. Am I not sending you?"
~ Judges 6:14

WHAT YOU NEED

- page 18, duplicated
- pencils
- red ¼-inch ribbon

BEFORE CLASS

Duplicate a pattern page for each child. Cut ribbon in 15-inch lengths. Roll a pattern page into a rolled paper and tie with a red ribbon to show the children.

WHAT TO DO

1. Introduce the lesson by telling the story of God's call to Gideon from Judges 6:1-24, 36-40. Ask, **What did God ask Gideon to do? How did Gideon know it was God who was asking him to do this?** Say, **Sometimes, God calls us to do jobs for Him too, and He will always help us do it.**
2. Distribute a pattern page to each child. Discuss the pictures on the page. Ask, **What job could each child do? Why might this be hard?**
3. Read the memory verse.
4. Ask students to write a job they could do for God on the page. Show them your rolled up paper. Help students roll and tie their papers with a strand of ribbon. Say, **When people are given a job to do, their job is written down and delivered to them. It is called a job description. You can pretend these are your orders from God. If your job seems too hard to do, remember that He is sending you and He wants to help you do it.**

EXTRA TIME

Play a relay race. Divide students into teams of four to six children on each team. Establish a track and space students along the track. Have students pass one of the rolled pages from person to person like a baton. Use a timer to see how quickly the team can pass the paper, then let the other teams have a try. Say, **When God gives us a job to do, it's important that we do what He says right away.**

What hard job can you do for God? Write about it below. Use the pictures as idea starters.

The Lord turned to him and said, "Go in the strength you have and save Israel out of Midian's hand. Am I not sending you?"
– Judges 6:14

God Helps Gideon Win a Battle

JUDGES 7:1-21

✓MEMORY VERSE

We trust in the name of the Lord our God.
~ Psalm 20:7

WHAT YOU NEED

- page 20, duplicated
- scissors
- pencils
- poster board or heavy card stock
- aluminum foil
- transparent tape
- glue

BEFORE CLASS

Duplicate a pattern page for each child. Make a sample craft to show the children.

WHAT TO DO

1. Ask, **If you arm wrestled with someone, who would probably win? The stronger person, right?** Introduce the lesson by telling the story from Judges 7:1-21. Say, **Gideon won the battle, not because he was stronger or had more men but because God helped him win. When we are in trouble God can help us because He is more powerful than we are and more powerful than whatever trouble we are facing.**
2. Show the children the sample craft.
3. Distribute a pattern page to each child. Read the memory verse together.
4. Have the children cut out the sword, then trace the sword on poster board. Instruct them to cut out the traced sword, cover the sword with aluminum foil, then glue the memory verse from the pattern page on top. Ask, **Do you ever have problems that seem too big to handle? How can you show that you trust God to help you?**

EXTRA TIME

Lead your children in brainstorming problems they might face, like a difficult friend, a grouchy parent, a dad out of work, or storm damage to their house. As you name each problem have students lift up their swords and shout the memory verse.

Five Minute

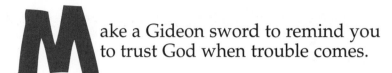

Make a Gideon sword to remind you to trust God when trouble comes.

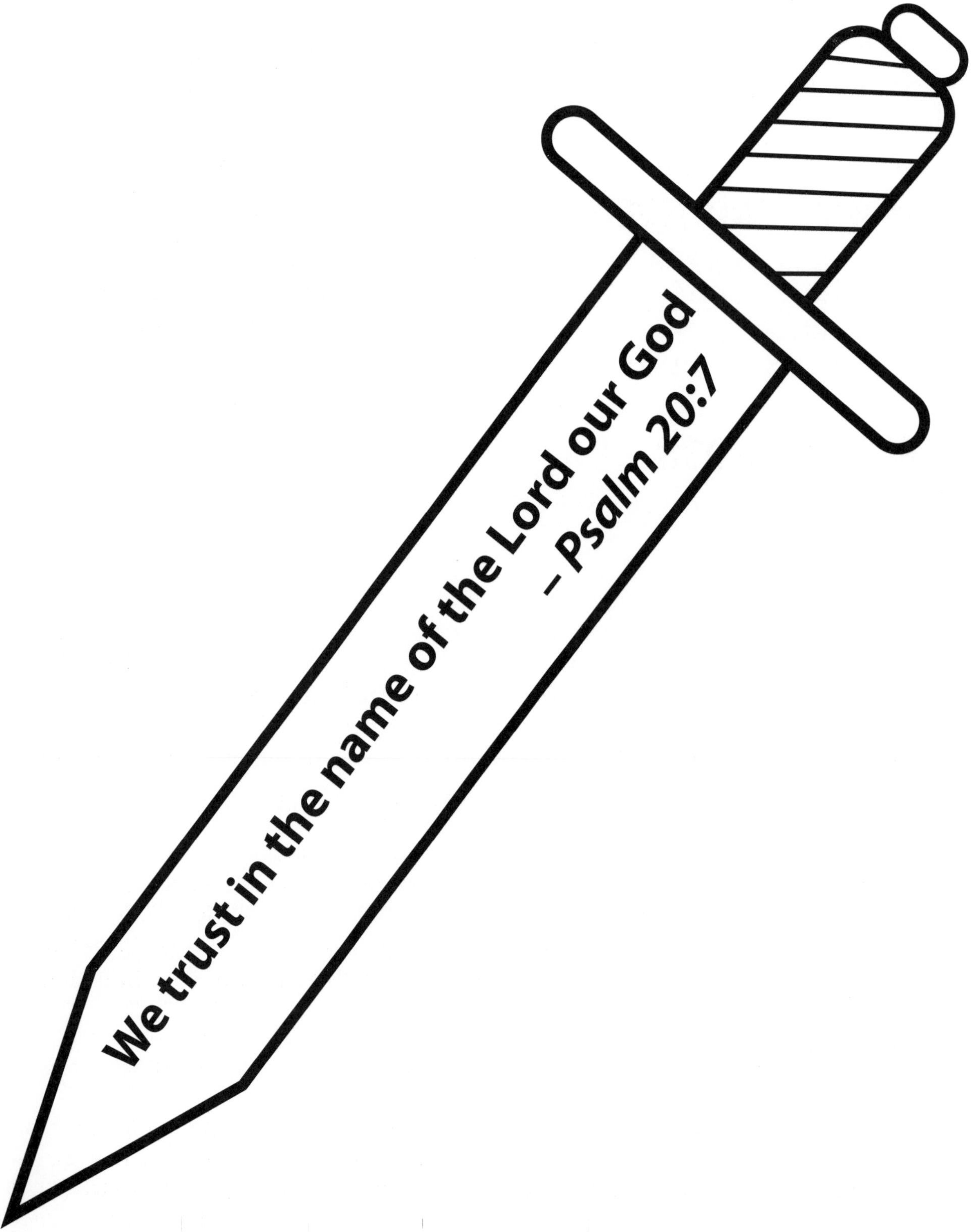
We trust in the name of the Lord our God
– Psalm 20:7

Samson Misuses His Gift
JUDGES 16:4-22

✓ MEMORY VERSE

The eyes of the Lord are on the righteous...
The face of the Lord is against those who do evil
~ Psalm 34:15, 16

WHAT YOU NEED

- page 22, duplicated
- paper plates
- glue
- yarn
- large craft sticks

BEFORE CLASS

Duplicate a pattern page for each child. Make a sample craft to show the children.

WHAT TO DO

1. Say, **God chose Samson to get rid of the Israelite's enemies. As long as Samson never cut his hair, he would have great strength so he could win over his enemies. Let's see how he used his strength.** Tell the story from Judges 16:4-22. Ask, **Was Samson right to tease Delilah then tell her why he was so strong? What happened to Samson because he told Delilah where his strength came from?**
2. Show the children the sample craft.
3. Distribute a pattern page to each child.
4. Say the memory verse.
5. Have the students cut out the face, glue it to the paper plate then glue strands of yarn on the back of the plate to make Samson's hair. Tell them to glue the craft stick to the base of the plate and attach the memory verse boxes, back to back, on the craft stick with the first half of the verse on the same side as the face.
6. Repeat the memory verse with the children. Say, **God will help us if we obey Him and do what He says. He will punish those who do wicked things. Samson treated his gift from God in a careless way, so God punished him.**

EXTRA TIME

Teach students to braid the hair on the back of the plate, braiding three strands at a time. Be sure to use longer strands of yarn if you have the students do the braiding.

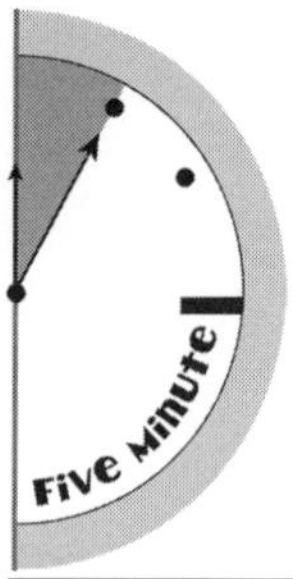

When Samson did right, God helped him. When Samson did wrong, God took his super strength away from him. Make a memory verse mask to tell what Samson did.

The eyes of the Lord are on the righteous.

The face of the Lord is against those who do evil.

– Psalm 34:15, 16

A Story About Sheep and Goats

MATTHEW 25:31-46

✓MEMORY VERSE

Whatever you did for one of the least of these brothers of mine, you did for me.
~ Matthew 25:40

WHAT YOU NEED

- page 24, duplicated
- pencils
- crayons

BEFORE CLASS

Duplicate a pattern page for each child. Solve the picture story to show the children.

WHAT TO DO

1. Present the story in sections. Tell the story from Matthew 25:31-39. Ask, **Who is talking? When did the people see Jesus in need?** Read Matthew 25:40. Then tell the story from Matthew 25:41-44. Ask, **What will Jesus' reply be?** Read Matthew 25:45,46. Say, **God will judge us by what we do for other people.**
2. Distribute a pattern page to each child.
3. Read the memory verse.
4. Show the sample picture story.
5. Instruct students to match the sentences and pictures by writing the right letter on each line, then color the pictures.
6. Ask, **If Jesus wants us to do these things for other people, what are some ways we can help hungry, sick or poor people or people who are in prison?**

EXTRA TIME

Discuss how your group can do a service project to aid people in need. Decorate a large box with pictures and symbols from the Bible story. Use the box to collect canned food or used clothing.

Finish the story to show how we can help Jesus. Use the pictures to help you finish each sentence.

I was hungry and you ☐

____

I was thirsty and you ☐

____

I was a stranger and you ☐

____

I needed clothes and you ☐

____

I was sick and you ☐

____

I was in prison and you ☐

____

Whatever you did for one of the least of these brothers of mine, you did for me.
– Matthew 25:40

The solution is on page 95.

Five Minute

The Israelites Want a King

1 SAMUEL 8

✓MEMORY VERSE

How awesome is the Lord Most High,
the great King over all the earth!
~ Psalm 47:2

WHAT YOU NEED

- page 26, duplicated
- pencils
- crayons

BEFORE CLASS

Duplicate a pattern page for each child.

WHAT TO DO

1. Introduce the lesson by telling the story from 1 Samuel 8. Ask, **Why did the Israelites want a king? Why did Samuel not want them to have a king?**
2. Distribute a pattern page to each child. Ask, **What does a king do?**
3. Ask the children to write or draw a story inside the large crown that tells what a king does.
4. Read the memory verse together.
5. Ask students to color the crowns that tell how God is like a king. Say, **Samuel thought the people should treat God like a king. God is our king because He rules over us. He is the ruler over everyone.**

EXTRA TIME

Have the children make paper crowns from construction paper, writing the memory verse on the front of the crown. Lead the children in a worship service where they pretend to give their crowns to God, saying the memory verse as they place the crowns on a table.

What is a king like? What does a king do? Write or draw your ideas inside the big crown.

How is God like a king? Color the crowns below that tell how God is like a king.

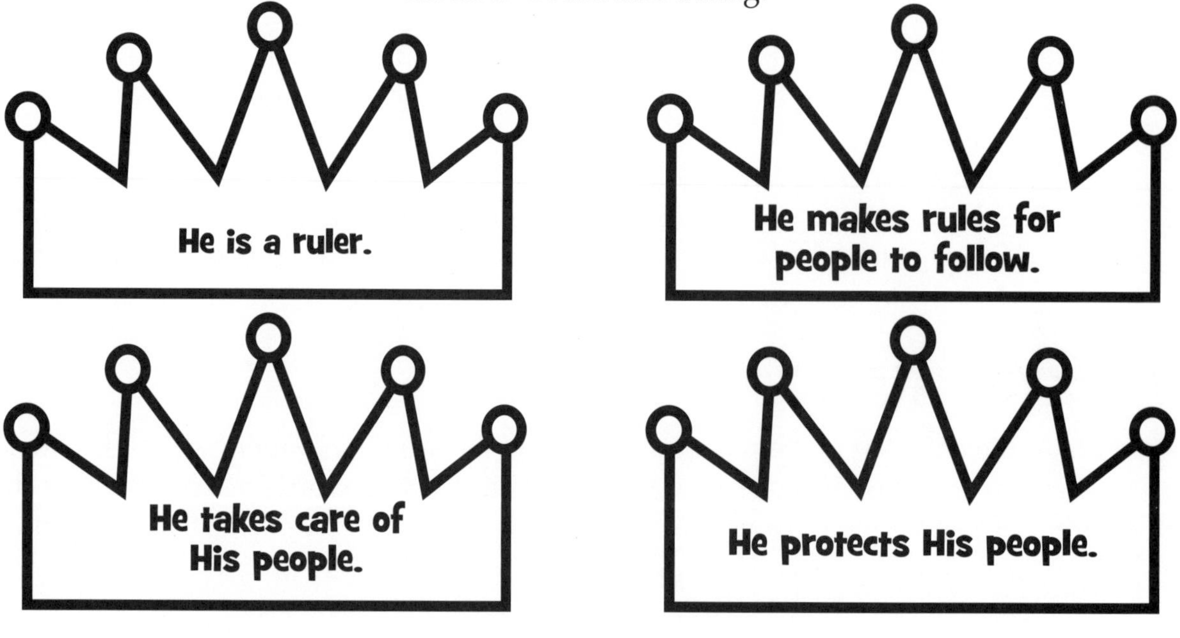

He is a ruler.
He makes rules for people to follow.
He takes care of His people.
He protects His people.

How awesome is the Lord Most High, the great King over all the earth!
– Psalm 47:2

The solution is on page 95.

Saul Becomes King

1 SAMUEL 9, 10:1-26

✓MEMORY VERSE

"For I know the plans I have for you," declares the Lord, "plans to prosper you and not to harm you, plans to give you hope and a future."
~ Jeremiah 29:11

WHAT YOU NEED

- page 28, duplicated
- pencils

BEFORE CLASS

Duplicate a pattern page for each child.

WHAT TO DO

1. Introduce the lesson by telling the story from 1 Samuel 9, 10:1-26. Read 1 Samuel 10:6, 7. Say, **Saul was just an ordinary young man. God changed him into a different kind of person so he would know how to be a good king.**
2. Distribute a pattern page to each child.
3. Say the memory verse together.
4. Direct students to complete the maze on the pattern page. Say, **When Saul went to look for his father's donkeys, he didn't know the plans God had for him. God has special plans for you too. If you follow him, He will be with you and make those plans happen.**

EXTRA TIME

Have students create their own maze on the other side of their pattern page, placing a picture of themselves at the beginning and a large question mark at the end of the maze. Write the memory verse on a white board so they can copy it on their paper. Say, **Our lives can take many twists and turns. You can't see what your life will turn out to be, but God can see and He knows the plans He has for you. You can be confident that He will do what is best for you.**

Five Minute

While looking for his father's donkeys, Saul found something else. Follow the maze to help Saul find what God had waiting for him.

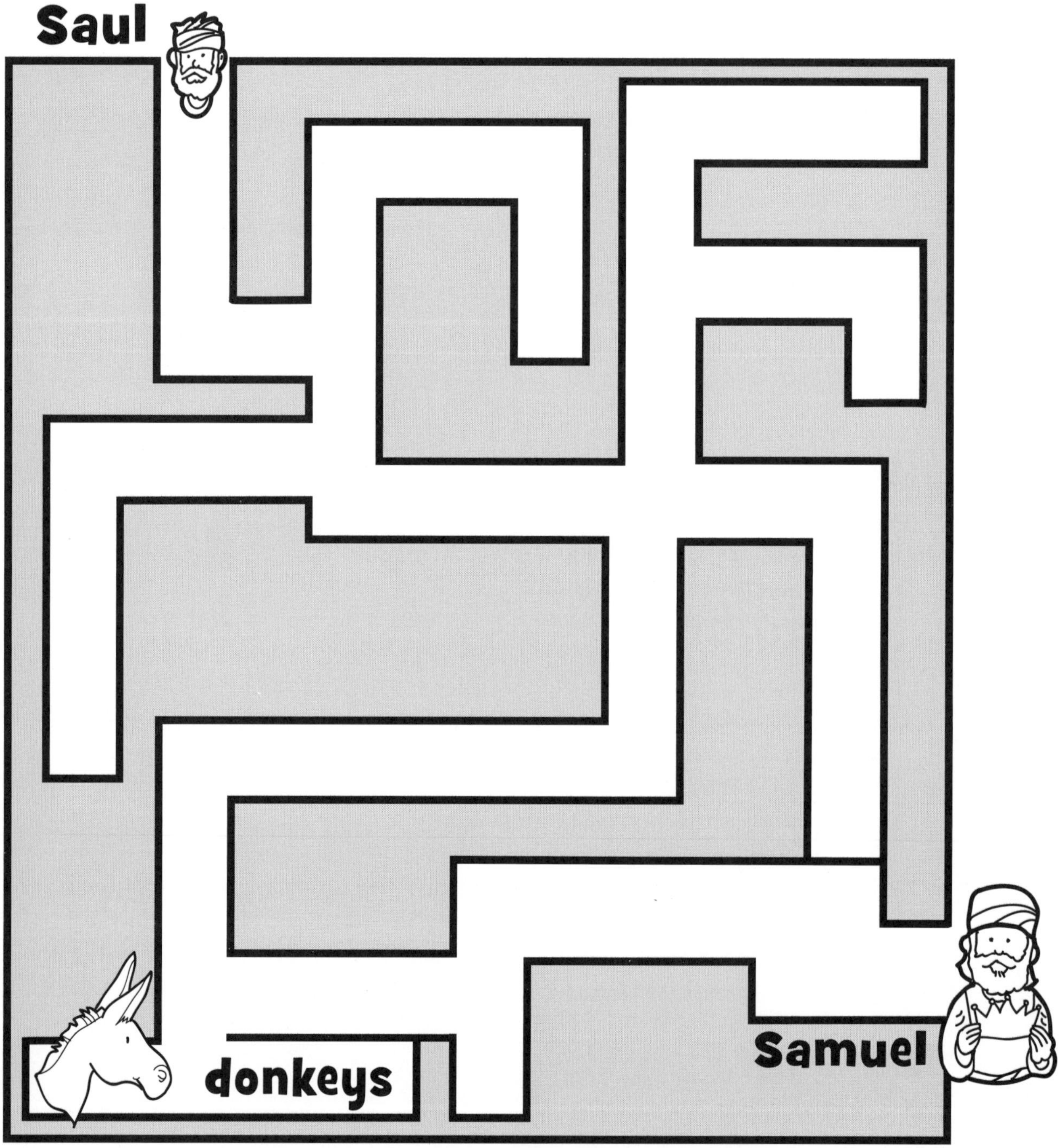

"For I know the plans I have for you," declares the Lord, "plans to prosper you and not to harm you, plans to give you hope and a future."
– Jeremiah 29:11

The solution is on page 95.

Saul Disobeys God

1 SAMUEL 13:1-14; 15:1-26

✓MEMORY VERSE

Walk in all the ways I command you,
that it may go well with you.
~ Jeremiah 7:23

WHAT YOU NEED

- page 30, duplicated
- crayons

BEFORE CLASS

Duplicate a pattern page for each child.

WHAT TO DO

1. Introduce the lesson by saying, **God chose Saul to be king, but twice Saul did not obey God's commands.** Tell the two stories from 1 Samuel 13:1-14 and 1 Samuel 15:1-26. Say, **Even though he was king, Saul still needed to obey God. Because Saul didn't obey God, God told Saul his sons could not be king after him.**
2. Distribute a pattern page to each child.
3. Say the memory verse.
4. Have students answer the questions by coloring in the stepping stones containing the answers to the three questions. Tell them to use the remaining words to complete the memory verse.
5. Repeat the memory verse together. Say, **No matter who we are or how important we are, all of us still need to obey what God tells us to do.**

EXTRA TIME

Make a hopscotch grid using tape if you are inside and sidewalk chalk if you can go outside. As students hop or step in each block or pair of blocks, have them say a word of the memory verse. Those who can successfully hop and step, and say the complete memory verse are the winners of the game.

Answer the questions below by coloring in the words in the path. Unscramble the uncolored words to complete the memory verse.

Color the following stones:

1. Two types of animals Saul didn't destroy?
2. Two things Saul didn't do that he was supposed to do?
3. Who told Saul to fight?

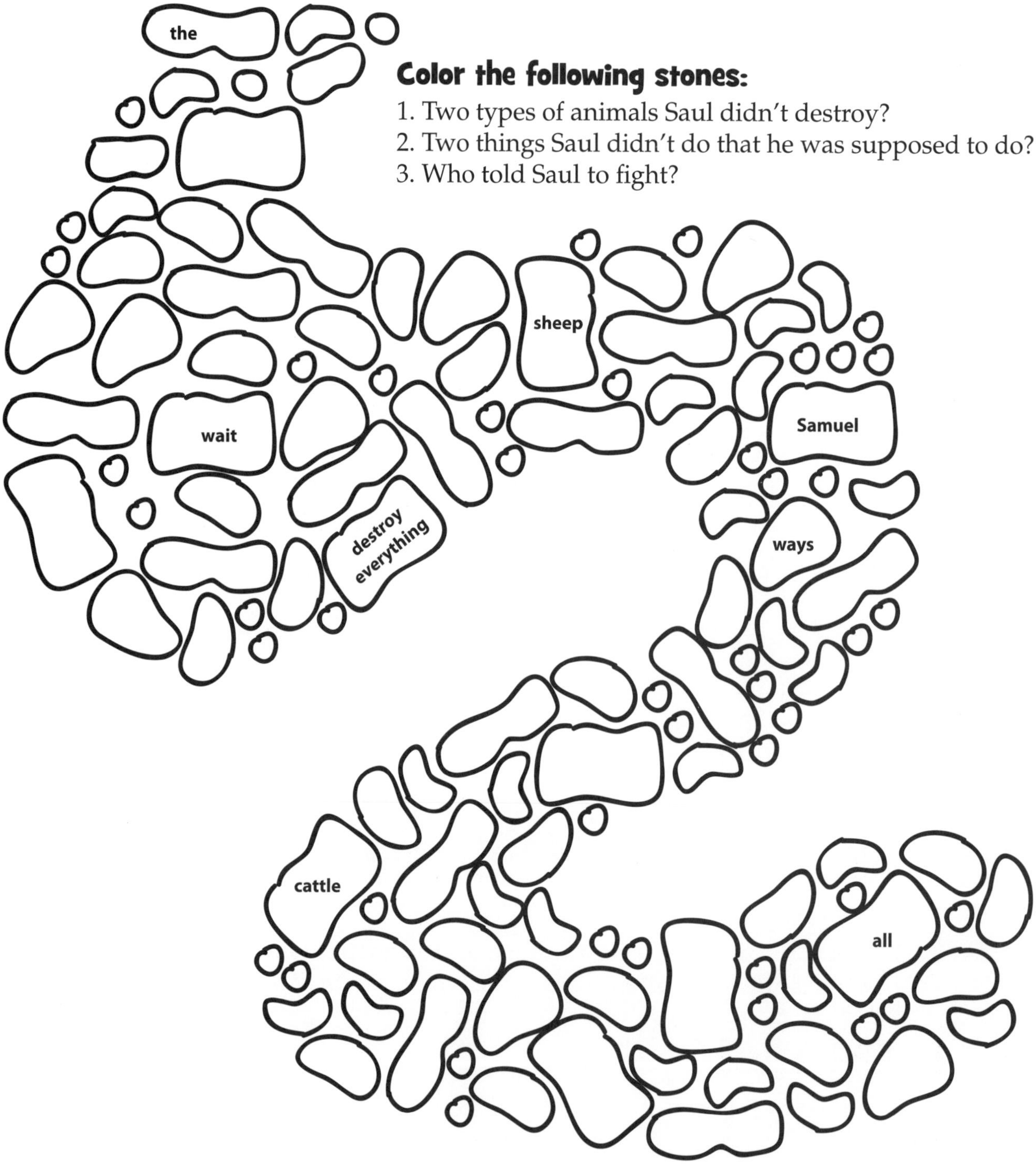

Walk in _______ ___________ __________ I command you, that it may go well with you.

– Jeremiah 7:23

The solution is on page 95.

Samuel Chooses David

1 SAMUEL 16:1-13

✓ MEMORY VERSE

The Lord does not look at the things man looks at. Man looks at the outward appearance but the Lord looks at the heart.
~ 1 Samuel 16:7

WHAT YOU NEED

- page 32, duplicated
- scissors
- crayons

BEFORE CLASS

Duplicate a pattern page for each child. Make a sample craft to show the children, drawing a picture of yourself on the outside paper doll.

WHAT TO DO

1. Introduce the lesson by telling the story from 1 Samuel 16:1-13. Say, **Samuel thought a strong, good looking young man would make a good king. But God was looking at what was on the inside, whether the future king would love and obey God. God cares more about what you think and how you act than what you look like.**
2. Show the sample craft to the children.
3. Distribute a pattern page to each child.
4. Say the memory verse. Have the children repeat it with you.
5. Guide the children in cutting out the paper dolls and folding them in half along the fold lines. Tell them to color a picture of themselves on the outside doll.
6. Say, **Many of us are just like Samuel. We want to judge people by how they look on the outside. But God cares about the kind of person you are on the inside.** Ask, **What kind of things would you like God to see inside you?** Have students write two or more ideas on the inside of their paper dolls.

EXTRA TIME

Brainstorm character traits that students would like to have God see inside of them. Lead the group in a circle prayer, having each child ask God to help them become the kind of person they would like to be.

What do people see when they look at you? What does God see? Draw a picture of yourself on the outside doll. Unfold the doll and draw or write what you would like God to see inside of you.

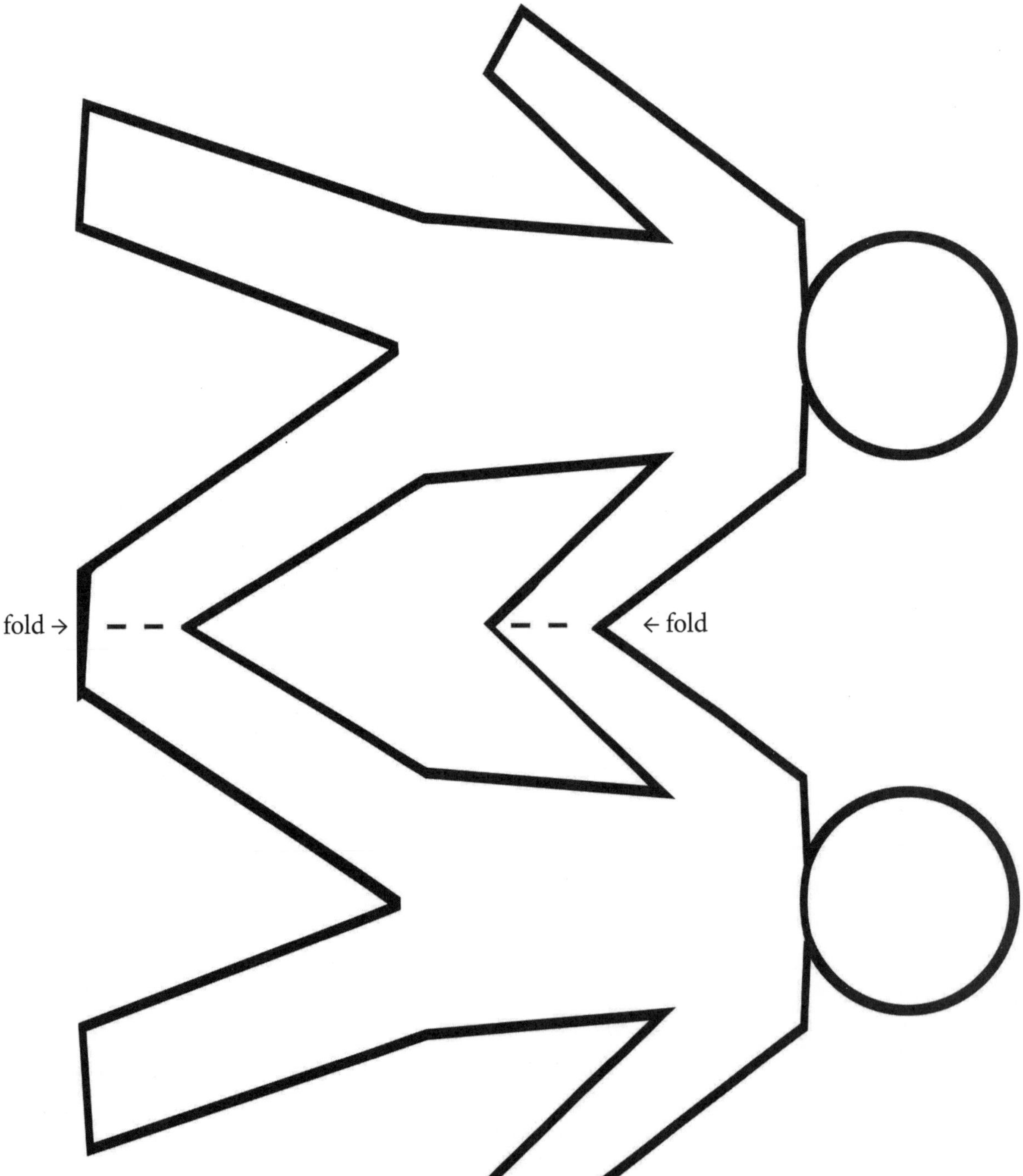

The Lord does not look at the things man looks at.
Man looks at the outward appearance, but the Lord looks at the heart.
- 1 Samuel 16:7

Saul is Jealous of David

1 SAMUEL 18:5-16; 19:1-10

✓MEMORY VERSE

Therefore encourage one another and build each other up.
~ 1 Thessalonians 5:11

WHAT YOU NEED

- page 34, duplicated
- crayons

BEFORE CLASS

Duplicate a pattern page for each child.

WHAT TO DO

1. Introduce the lesson by telling the Bible story from 1 Samuel 18:5-16; 19:1-10. Say, **David became more popular and successful than King Saul. Saul didn't like that. Saul became so jealous that he wanted to do harm to David.**
2. Distribute a pattern page to each child.
3. Say the memory verse. Ask, **What should we do instead of being jealous of a friend's success?** Listen to several answers, guiding the children to mention encouraging others.
4. Guide the children in coloring the circles of ways to respond to a successful friend. Ask, **What could Saul have done differently instead of being jealous?**

EXTRA TIME

Have students make encouragement cards. Have them write encouraging words on 1 x 2 inch pieces of card stock, such as "Good job," "Way to go," "Congrats," "You were great," or "That was awesome!" Provide stickers and markers for decorating the cards. Encourage the children to keep the cards in a school notebook or lunch box to hand out to their friends when their friends are successful.

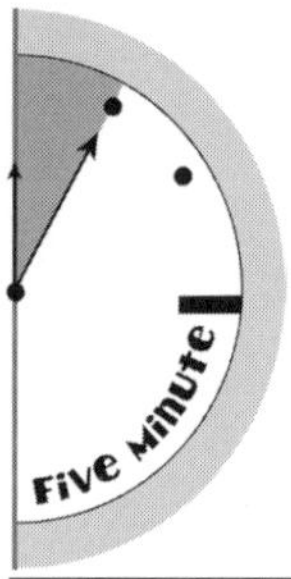

Color the circles that describe how God wants you to react when a friend is more successful than you.

When someone else does better than me, I will:

- Tell them they did a good job.
- Talk nasty about them to other people.
- Cheat off his or her test.
- Pray for them.
- Work harder to do better than them.
- Steal their award.
- Tell them how they messed up.
- Tell someone else what a good job they did.
- Work harder to do my best.
- Make up lies about them.

Therefore, encourage one another and build each other up.
– 1 Thessalonians 5:11

The solution is on page 95.

David Spares Saul's Life

1 SAMUEL 24

✓MEMORY VERSE

Love your enemies, do good to those who hate you.
~ Luke 6:27

WHAT YOU NEED

- page 36, duplicated
- pencils
- crayons

BEFORE CLASS

Duplicate a pattern page for each child.

WHAT TO DO

1. Introduce the lesson by telling the story from 1 Samuel 24. Say, **David's friends tried to get him to kill Saul because Saul was chasing him. David did not kill Saul because Saul was God's choice for king and David knew God would protect him.**
2. Distribute a pattern page to each child.
3. Say the memory verse.
4. Tell the children to match the pictures by drawing a line from each "before" picture on the top row to the corresponding "after" picture on the bottom row. Ask them to draw their own pictures of how they can do good to someone who has been mean to them. Say, **We are able to love those who are mean to us because we know God will take care of us just like David knew God would protect him.** Repeat the memory verse together.

EXTRA TIME

Have the children use fabric pens to write the memory verse on large square pieces of felt. If you have a group of younger children, have them paint only the first phrase. Write out the letters with a pencil beforehand for them to trace over.

Five Minute

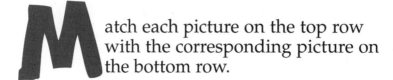

Match each picture on the top row with the corresponding picture on the bottom row.

How has someone been mean to you? How can you do good for them?
Draw your set of pictures here.

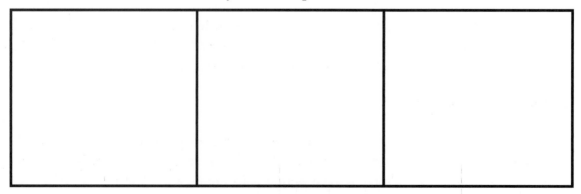

Love your enemies. Do good to those who hate you.
– Luke 6:27

The solution is on page 95.

David is Kind to Mephibosheth

2 SAMUEL 9

✓MEMORY VERSE

Make sure that nobody pays back wrong for wrong, but always try to be kind to each other and to everyone else.
~ 1 Thessalonians 5:15

WHAT YOU NEED

- page 38, duplicated
- Bibles
- pencils

BEFORE CLASS

Duplicate a pattern page for each child.

WHAT TO DO

1. Introduce the lesson by telling the story from 2 Samuel 9. Say, **Mephibosheth was Saul's grandson. Most people would not bother being kind to the relatives of a former king. But David was kind because it was the right thing to do.**
2. Distribute a pattern page and a Bible to each child.
3. Have the children try to find and circle the missing words in the word puzzle and fill in the blanks. Help them find 1 Thessalonians 5:15 in their Bibles to check their work.
4. Repeat the memory verse together. Say, **God, our King, wants us to be kind too. What are some ways we can show kindness to other people?** Ask children to draw their idea at the bottom of the page.

EXTRA TIME

Have students make small bouquets with silk flowers, ribbon, and an attached note that says, "Have a great day!" Encourage the children to give their flowers to someone who needs friendship.

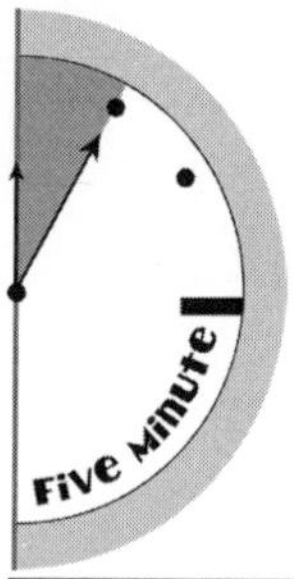

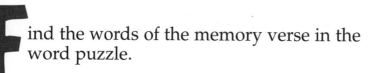

Find the words of the memory verse in the word puzzle.

S	U	R	E	J	W	X	V	L	P
W	L	P	N	M	V	Z	S	G	J
R	E	K	X	R	J	K	Y	O	P
O	R	I	Z	E	D	S	G	H	K
N	Q	N	O	A	F	C	U	K	L
G	E	D	C	T	R	T	Y	H	J
P	T	E	A	C	H	F	G	K	T
X	V	Z	N	O	T	H	E	R	O
E	L	S	E	S	N	A	I	T	H

Make ________________ that nobody pays back ________________ for wrong,
but always try to be ___________ to ____________ ____________,
and to everyone ____________.

– 1 Thessalonians 5:15

How can you be kind to someone?

____

The solution is on page 95.

Absalom Tries to Become King

2 SAMUEL 15:1-18, 18:1-17

✓ MEMORY VERSE

The Lord is King for ever and ever.
~ Psalm 10:16

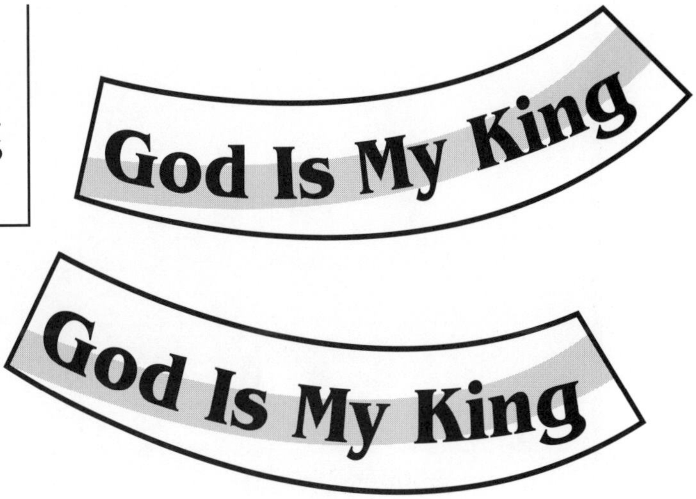

WHAT YOU NEED

- page 40, duplicated
- scissors
- construction paper
- glue
- crayons

BEFORE CLASS

Duplicate a pattern page for each child. Make a sample craft to show the children.

WHAT TO DO

1. Introduce the lesson by telling the story from 2 Samuel 15:1-18, 18:1-17. Say, **David was the lawful king, chosen by God. Absalom tried to become king on his own. God is our King. He rules over us and He makes rules for us to follow. When we try to live life the way we want, we are like Absalom. We are trying to be king over our lives instead of honoring God as our king.**
2. Show the sample craft to the children.
3. Distribute a pattern page and construction paper to each child.
4. Say the memory verse.
5. Say, **We're going to make banners that tell that God is our king.** Have students cut out the banner. Have them cut a piece of construction paper in half, then tape the two pieces of banner and construction paper together. Have them glue the banner on the construction paper. Allow them to color and decorate the banner if there is time remaining.

EXTRA TIME

Lead the children in singing praise songs that emphasize God's place as ruler and King.

Make a banner to tell everyone that God is your king.

God Is

My King

The Lord is King for ever and ever.
– Psalm 10:16

Elijah and the Widow

1 KINGS 17:7-24

✓MEMORY VERSE

Then they cried to the Lord in their trouble, and He saved them from their distress.
~ Psalm 107:13

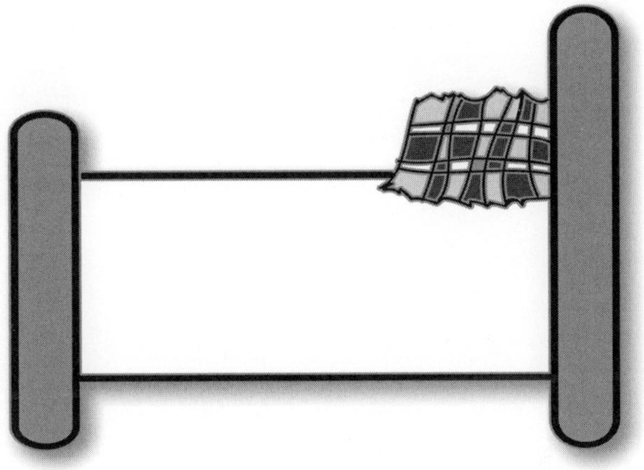

WHAT YOU NEED

- page 42, duplicated
- pencils
- small craft sticks
- 1-inch fabric squares
- glue
- scissors

BEFORE CLASS

Duplicate a pattern page for each child. Make a sample craft to show the children.

WHAT TO DO

1. Introduce the lesson by telling the story from 1 Kings 17:7-24, emphasizing the section about the widow's son. Ask, **How did Elijah help the widow and her son? What did Elijah do when the little boy died?** Say, **Elijah cried out to the Lord. God made the boy live again. When we face trouble, we can ask God for help, too.**
2. Show the sample craft to the children.
3. Distribute a pattern page to each child.
4. Have the children say the memory verse with you.
5. Ask, **Do you know someone who is very sick or is in trouble?** Ask the children to write the name of someone they would like to pray for inside the bed. Have the children cut out the bed, glue small craft sticks for legs of the bed and a fabric square for a pillow. Say, **Put your special bed in a place you can see so you can remember to pray every day for the person you've written down.**

EXTRA TIME

Have a prayer circle. Give each child who is willing a chance to pray out loud for the person they have written on their craft.

Do you know someone who needs God's help? Write their name on the bed then pray for them. Watch for what God will do!

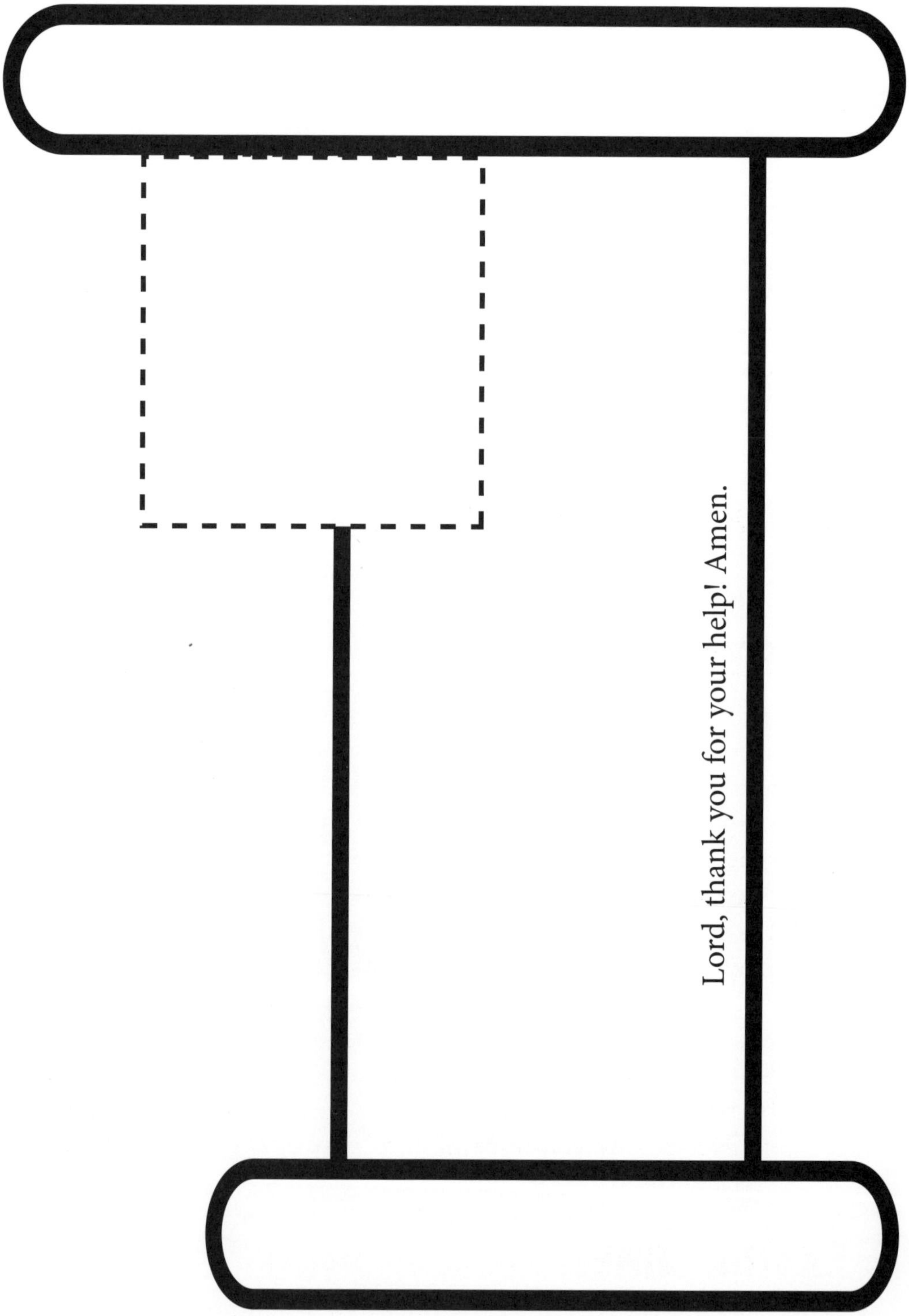
Lord, thank you for your help! Amen.

Then they cried to the Lord in their trouble and He saved them from their distress.
– Psalm 107:13

Elijah at Mount Carmel

1 KINGS 18:16-39

Five Minute

✓MEMORY VERSE

Acknowledge and take to heart this day that the Lord is God in heaven above and on the earth below. There is no other.
~ Deuteronomy 4:39

WHAT YOU NEED

- page 44, duplicated
- construction paper
- scissors
- glue sticks
- crayons

BEFORE CLASS

Duplicate a pattern page for each child. Make a sample craft to show the children.

WHAT TO DO

1. Introduce the lesson by telling the story from 1 Kings 18:16-39. Say, **Hundreds of prophets believed Baal was a god. The people were confused and didn't know whether to worship Baal or the one true God. Elijah had to show the people that God was the only God. There is only one real God, and we should worship only Him.**
2. Distribute a pattern page to each child.
3. Say the memory verse. Have the group repeat it with you.
4. Show the children the sample craft.
5. Instruct them to cut out the pictures and arrange them on construction paper to show what happened when Elijah prayed. They can color the pictures and add story details to the construction paper as time allows. Have students take turns telling the story, using their pictures as a story aid. Say, **There is only one true God, and we need to be willing to talk to people about Him.**

EXTRA TIME

Lead the group in a choral response. Line the children in a line facing you. Choose one child to face the entire group and shout, "The Lord is God." Have the entire group respond, "There is no other!' Choose a new child to stand before the group and lead the choral response.

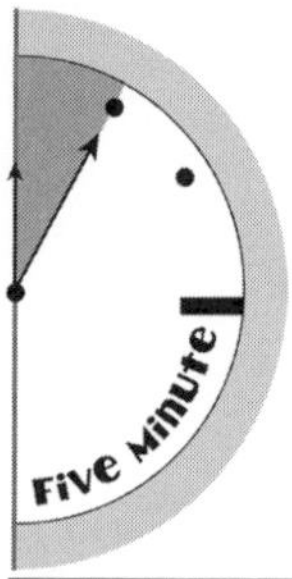

Cut out and glue the pictures below on construction paper to create a story picture about Elijah at Mount Carmel.

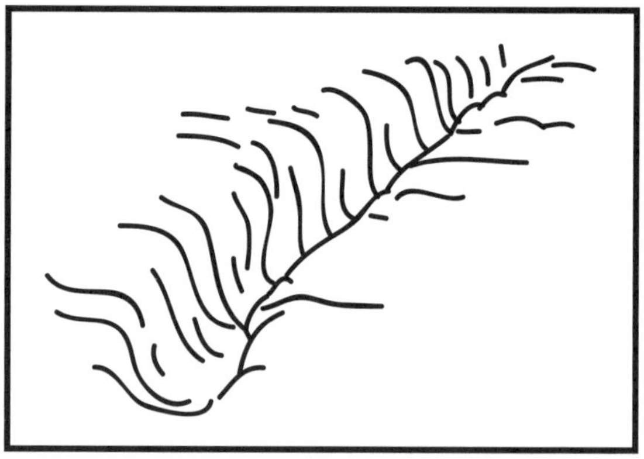

Acknowledge and take to heart this day that the Lord is God in heaven above and on the earth below. There is no other.
– Deuteronomy 4:39

Naboth's Vineyard
1 KINGS 21

✓MEMORY VERSE

He will judge the world in righteousness;
he will govern the peoples with justice.
~ Psalm 9:8

WHAT YOU NEED

- page 46, duplicated
- crayons
- scissors
- stapler

BEFORE CLASS

Duplicate a pattern page for each child. Make a sample craft to show the children.

WHAT TO DO

1. Introduce the lesson by telling the story of Naboth's vineyard from 1 Kings 21. Say, **Even though he was king, Ahab did not have the right to kill Naboth for his vineyard. God punished Ahab for his wicked deed.**
2. Show the sample craft to the children.
3. Distribute a pattern page to each child.
4. Introduce the memory verse. Say, **When someone does something wrong to you, God sees and knows and God will do what is right for you.**
5. Have the children put the story pictures in the right order by placing a number from one to six in the upper left hand corner of each picture. Have them color the pictures, cut them out and place them in the right order according to the numbers. Help them staple the pages together to make a story book. Say, **Ahab did a very wrong thing. If we keep doing what is wrong, God will punish us. He is God the King and He expects us to follow His commandments.**

EXTRA TIME

Act out the story of Ahab and Naboth. Choose children to play the parts of Ahab, Jezebel, Naboth, the accusers and Elijah. Use the pattern page for the story book to prompt the children's memories if needed.

Number the pictures in the right order, Color and cut out the pictures to make a story book.

He will judge the world in righteousness; he will govern the people with justice.
– Psalm 9:8

The solution is on page 96.

Elisha and the Widow's Oil

2 KINGS 4:1-7

✓MEMORY VERSE

And my God will meet all your needs according to His glorious riches in Christ Jesus.
~ Philippians 4:19

WHAT YOU NEED

- page 48, duplicated
- pencils
- crayons

BEFORE CLASS

Duplicate a pattern page for each child.

WHAT TO DO

1. Introduce the lesson by telling the story from 2 Kings 4:1-7. Ask, **If the widow only had five jars, how much oil would she have had? If she had twenty jars, how much oil would she have had?**
2. Distribute a pattern page to each child.
3. Ask students to find the word missing from the memory verse and write it in the blank. Say the memory verse together. Say, **God owns everything in the world. He can provide you with more than you need. All you need to do is ask Him for what you need.**
4. Have students draw pictures of items they need, such as clothes, shoes, money, food, and water inside the jars. Say, **If our family has a special need for something like a new house, a new washing machine, or money to fix the car, we can ask God for His help.**

EXTRA TIME

Let your children experience how the widow felt as she poured oil into the jar. Have students squirt water from a full water bottle into small paper cups to see how many cups they can fill before running out of water. Say, **The widow didn't run out of oil until she ran out of containers! God made sure there was enough oil for all those jars.**

What do you need? Draw the items you need inside the jars. Look for the word missing from the memory verse inside one of the jars.

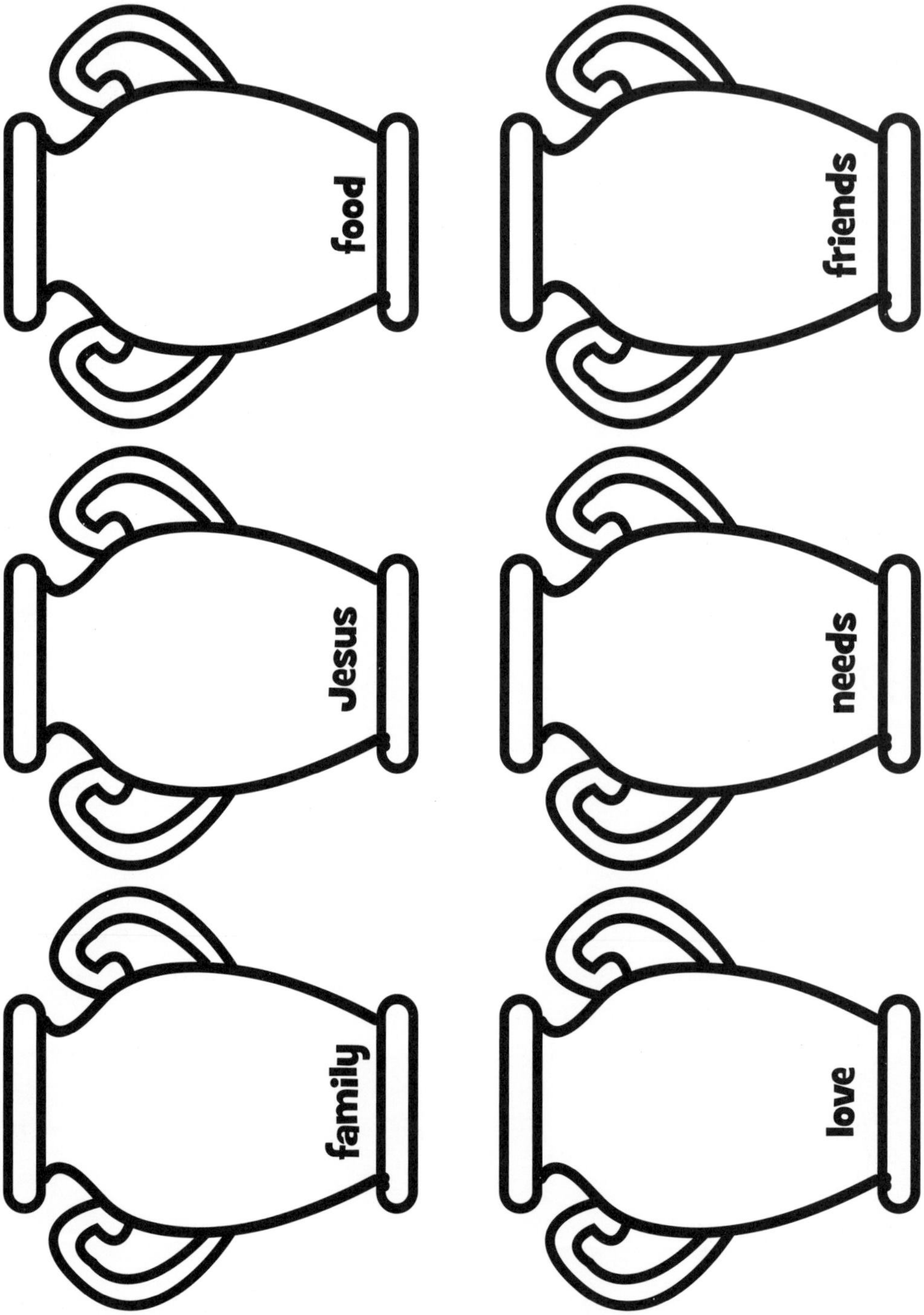

And my God will meet all your ____________________________ according to His glorious riches in Christ Jesus.
– Philippians 4:19

The solution is on page 96.

Elisha and the Army of God

2 KINGS 6:8-23

✓MEMORY VERSE

The angel of the Lord encamps around those who fear Him, and He delivers them.
~ Psalm 34:7

WHAT YOU NEED

- page 50, duplicated
- crayons
- pencils

BEFORE CLASS

Duplicate a pattern page for each child.

WHAT TO DO

1. Introduce the lesson by telling the story from 2 Kings 6:8-23. Ask, **What did Elisha's servant see at first? What did Elisha see? Did the servant need to be afraid of the enemy's army? Why not?**
2. Distribute a pattern page to each child. Ask the children to write their name in the center circle.
3. Discuss things that the children in your class fear could harm them. Ask them to write or draw those things in the space between the two circles..
4. Ask students to put a finger at the starting point on the outside circle. Ask them to cross out every other letter in the circle, then write the remaining letters on the lines below the circle.
5. When someone completes the puzzle, ask them to read the verse to you. Explain that the word "encamps" means "surrounds." Say, **God protects us so well that it's like He is surrounding us on every side. If God is surrounding you, can anything harm you?**

EXTRA TIME

Make signs for some of the things your students fear. Ask everyone to stand in a circle. Tell them they are the army of God. Ask several volunteers to stand inside the circle, holding the signs. Ask another volunteer to stand in the middle of the circle. Have those with signs shout what their signs say, while those on the outside shout the memory verse together. Ask your solo volunteer which group is stronger.

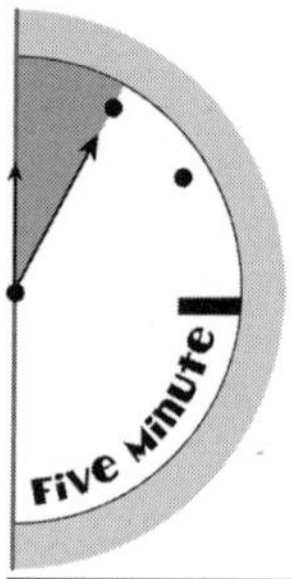

Write your name in the center of the circle. Draw pictures of things that could hurt you in the middle circle. Cross out every other letter after the circled "T" in the outside circle to find out why you don't need to be afraid.

TxhvekaznjgqewlcopfztyhqemLpowrxdvebnfcraemspdszawrqoruknldwtrhtoysgehwkhjoxfresawrdHbiumpagnjdzHxewdreqlzisvkejrwsytrhtexmb

your name

___ ___ ___ ___

___ ___

___ ___ ___

___ ___ ___ ___, ___ ___

___ ___ ___ ___. – Psalm 34:7

The solution is on page 96.

The Shunammite Woman Gets Her Land Back

2 KINGS 4:8-36; 8:1-6

✓MEMORY VERSE

Your Father knows what you need before you ask him.
~ Matthew 6:8

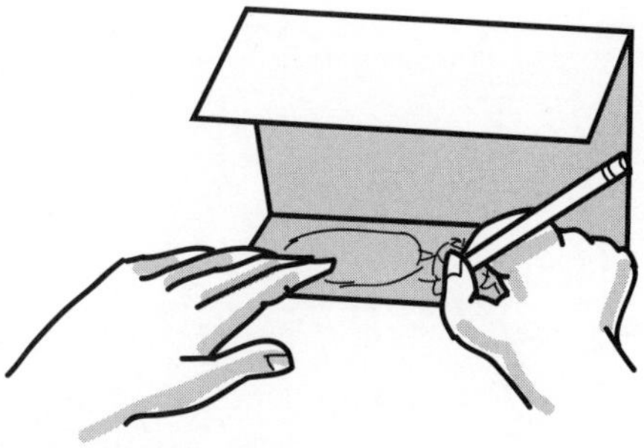

WHAT YOU NEED

- page 52, duplicated
- pencils
- large poster board
- wide tipped poster marker

BEFORE CLASS

Duplicate a pattern page for each child. Make a sample craft to show the children. Write the memory verse on a large poster board

WHAT TO DO

1. Introduce the lesson by telling the Bible story. Briefly explain the story background from 2 Kings 4:8-36, focusing mostly on the details of 2 Kings 8:1-6. Say, **The woman didn't know that Elisha's servant was there when she went to see the king about her land. If the servant had not been talking about the wonderful things God had done for her, the king may not have been as willing to give her land back to her.**
2. Show the poster with the memory verse. Ask, **Did God know the woman needed her land back? How did God help her?**
3. Show the sample craft to the children and distribute pattern pages.
4. Have students fold the page on the dotted lines so the pictures are on the outside. Have students open the flaps and copy the memory verse on the inside. Allow students to color the pictures as time allows.

EXTRA TIME

Make folded prayer cards. Fold index cards in half. Have the children write a prayer request on the outside flap, then write the memory verse reference on the inside. Have students repeat the verse from memory. Say, **This verse will help you remember when you are asking God for something, that even if you don't see Him answer your prayer right away, He knows your need and He is working on it in ways you may not even see.**

Make a folding story scene. Fold on the dotted lines. Inside, write the memory verse. When does God know what you need?

Tell me about the great things Elisha has done.

This is the woman, my lord the king, and this is her son whom Elisha restored to life.

Joash Repairs the Temple

2 CHRONICLES 24:1-14

✓ MEMORY VERSE

All the officials and all the people brought their contributions gladly, dropping them into the chest until it was full.
~ 2 Chronicles 24:10

WHAT YOU NEED

- page 54, duplicated
- pencils
- crayons

BEFORE CLASS

Duplicate a pattern page for each child.

WHAT TO DO

1. Ask, **Does your house ever need to be cleaned? Do things ever break in your house?** Introduce the lesson by telling the story from 2 Chronicles 24:1-14. Say, **People had not taken care of the temple for years. Parts of the building needed repair. But the repairs cost money. The people were willing to give them money so the temple could be fixed.**
2. Distribute a pattern page to each child.
3. Say the memory verse.
4. Tell the children to find and circle objects and jobs in the picture that cost money. When finished, they may color the page. Say, **Everything done at a church costs money. When you give your money to the church, the leaders use it to keep the church looking nice and to do God's work so people will know about God.**

EXTRA TIME

Role play a church job career day. On sticky notes, ask children to write down various jobs people can do for a church, one job per sticky note. Have children attach a job to their shirt and introduce themselves to others while "in character." They may also trade church jobs with others.

Circle the things your offering money can help do for your church.

All the officials and all the people brought their contributions gladly, dropping them into the chest until it was full.
– 2 Chronicles 24:10

Hezekiah Prays for His Country

2 KINGS 18:17-19:19, 35,36

✓MEMORY VERSE

If my people... will humble themselves and pray and seek my face and turn from their wicked ways, then will I hear from heaven and will forgive their sin and will heal their land.
~ 2 Chronicles 7:14

WHAT YOU NEED

- page 56, duplicated
- crayons
- pencils
- tape or glue
- large pieces of construction paper

BEFORE CLASS

Duplicate a pattern page for each child. Make a sample craft to show the children.

WHAT TO DO

1. Introduce the lesson by telling the story from 2 Kings 18:17-19:19,35-36. Say, **Enemies attacked Hezekiah's country. Hezekiah's solution was to pray and ask God to help them. God wants us to pray about the problems we have in our country, too.**
2. Show the sample craft to the children.
3. Distribute a pattern page to each child.
4. Say the memory verse.
5. Help the children fill in the blanks with names of the current president, governor of your state, mayor of your city, their school principal's name, a name of someone in the military that you know, and a problem the country, your town, or a school is currently facing that the children know about. Have the children color the page, then glue it to the construction paper. Say, **If we have problems in our country, town, or school, we can ask God for help and He will help us.**

EXTRA TIME

Help the children hang their posters in prominent places around the building or in other public places. Arrange to have a prayer circle near one of the posters to pray for the country and its leaders.

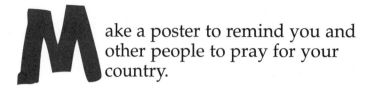

Make a poster to remind you and other people to pray for your country.

____

President

____

Governor

God wants YOU to pray for your country

____

Mayor

____

School Principal

____

Someone in the Military

____

What my country needs now

If my people... will humble themselves and pray
and seek my face and turn from their wicked ways,
then will I hear from heaven and will forgive their sin and will heal their land.
– 2 Chronicles 7:14

God Spares Hezekiah's Life

2 KINGS 20:1-11

✓MEMORY VERSE

The living, the living—they praise you, as I am doing today.
~ Isaiah 38:19

WHAT YOU NEED

- page 58, duplicated
- scissors
- paper plates
- paper fasteners
- glue
- markers
- construction paper

BEFORE CLASS

Duplicate a pattern page for each child. Make a sample craft to show the children.

WHAT TO DO

1. Introduce the lesson by telling the story from 2 Kings 20:1-11. Say, **God proved to Hezekiah He would heal him by making time go backwards. Hezekiah praised God because he knew God was the one who kept him from dying and gave him fifteen more years of life. Whenever God answers our prayers, it's important to thank Him right away.**
2. Show the sample craft to the children.
3. Distribute a pattern page to each child. Say the memory verse together.
5. Ask students to draw two or three things for which they are thankful on the clock face. Direct students to cut out the clock face, glue it on a paper plate, then attach construction paper hands to the clock with a paper fastener. Say, **We don't have to wait for a specific time to pray. You can thank God for what He has done for you any time!**

EXTRA TIME

Play the alphabet game. Seat your students in a circle. The first person says, "I praise God today. I am thankful for..." then names something that begins with the letter *A*. The next person on the right repeats the sentence, then adds something that begins with the letter *B*. Play continues until everyone has had a turn or you run out of letters.

Five Minute

God is working all the time so you can thank Him anytime. Make a clock. Draw pictures on your clock of what you can thank God for.

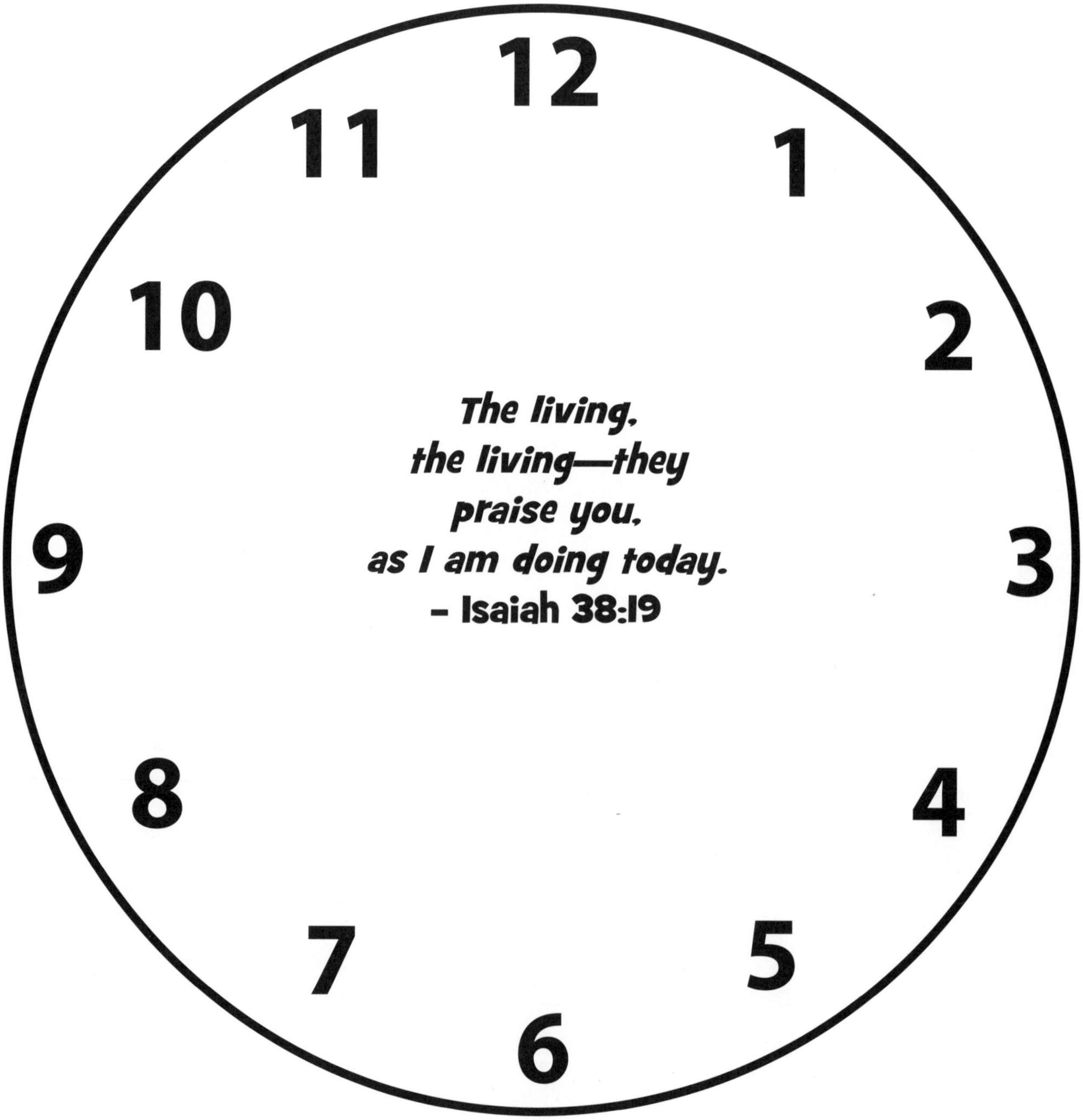
12
1
2
3
4
5
6
7
8
9
10
11
The living,
the living—they
praise you,
as I am doing today.
- Isaiah 38:19

Hezekiah Becomes Proud

2 KINGS 20:12-19, 2 CHRONICLES 32:24-29

✓MEMORY VERSE

Give thanks to the Lord, call on his name; make known among the nations what he has done.
~ Psalm 105:1

WHAT YOU NEED

- page 60, duplicated
- scissors
- crayons or markers
- 3-inch square cardboard boxes with lids
- glue sticks

BEFORE CLASS

Duplicate a pattern page for each child. Make a sample craft to show the children.

WHAT TO DO

1. Introduce the lesson by telling the story from 2 Kings 20:12-19 and 2 Chronicles 32:24-29. Say, **Instead of telling his visitors how God had miraculously healed him, Hezekiah showed them all the wealth he had and the things he had done. God doesn't want us to be proud and say, "Look what I've done." God wants us to give Him the credit for what He has done for us.**
2. Show the sample craft to the children.
3. Distribute a pattern page to each child. Repeat the memory verse together.
4. Work together to brainstorm ways to complete the sentences. Have children write or draw their ideas in each square.
5. Tell children to cut apart the four squares, glue the memory verse box to the lid top, then fold the other three squares and place inside the box. Say, **Hezekiah showed his visitors many of his treasures. Your treasure box can remind you of what God has done for you.**

EXTRA TIME

Provide markers, acrylic paint, glitter, sequins, and fabric for children to decorate the outside of their treasure boxes.

Five Minute

Make a treasure box to remind you of what God has done for you. In the last square tell about what God did for someone you care about.

Give thanks to the Lord, call on his name; make known among the nations what he has done. **– Psalm 105:1**	**God gave me** ________________ ________________ ________________
God did this for me ________________ ________________ ________________	**I saw God do this for__________** ________________ ________________ ________________

Manasseh is Sorry for His Sin

2 CHRONICLES 33:1-20

✓MEMORY VERSE

Repent, then, and turn to God, so that your sins may be wiped out, that times of refreshing may come from the Lord. ~ Acts 3:19

WHAT YOU NEED

- page 62, duplicated
- markers
- scissors
- craft sticks
- glue or tape

BEFORE CLASS

Duplicate a pattern page for each child. Make a sample craft to show the children.

WHAT TO DO

1. Introduce the lesson by telling the story from 2 Chronicles 33:1-20. Say, **Manasseh did evil things. He told God he was sorry, then stopped doing those wrong things. What did he do that was right?**
2. Show the sample craft to the children.
3. Distribute a pattern page to each child. Say the memory verse.
4. Have the children color and cut out the puppets, then glue the two puppets back to back with the craft stick between them. Tell the story again. As you reach the part of the story where Manasseh repents, have the children turn their puppets to face the other way. Say, **Manasseh repented. To repent means to stop doing evil, say you are sorry to God, and start doing what is good. It's like deciding to stop going one direction, turning around and going another direction, toward God and what He wants.**
6. Repeat the memory verse together.

EXTRA TIME

Work with your group to create a large U-turn sign out of yellow poster board and black crepe paper or construction paper. Have the group take turns walking on the U-turn, naming things children do that are wrong, such as using bad words. When they reach the bend, have them repeat the memory verse, then name a way that person could change; for example, don't say bad words anymore.

Make a puppet of Manasseh so you can tell the story. Use your puppet to show how Manasseh turned around when he was sorry for his sins.

Repent, then, and turn to God, so that your sins may be wiped out, that times of refreshing may come from the Lord.
– Acts 3:19

Josiah Finds the Book of the Law

2 CHRONICLES 34:1-32

✓MEMORY VERSE

But his delight is in the law of the Lord,
and on his law he meditates day and night.
~ Psalm 1:2

WHAT YOU NEED

- page 64, duplicated
- large sheets of construction paper
- glue sticks

BEFORE CLASS

Duplicate a pattern page for each child. Make a sample craft to show the children.

WHAT TO DO

1. Introduce the lesson by telling the story from 2 Chronicles 34:1-32. Say, **Josiah wanted to obey God's law. He wanted his people to obey God's law too. He read the book of the Law to all the people so they would know how to obey God. We need to read the Bible too, so we know how to obey God.**
2. Show the sample craft. Say, **Today we're going to make a Bible Reading Plan poster.**
3. Distribute a pattern page to each child.
4. Say the memory verse, which is the first verse listed on the Bible Reading Plan.
5. Have the children glue the pattern page to a sheet of construction paper. Have students take turns reading the different verses. Say, **Take this reading plan home and hang it in your room where you can see it. Every day, read the Bible verse for that day. When you read the Bible, you will find out how to obey God. He wants you to love reading His words in the Bible.**

EXTRA TIME

Help your students locate the verses on their Bible reading plan in a Bible. If students have brought their own Bibles, help them mark the pages of each verse with a mini sticky note.

Take this reading plan home and hang it in your room where you can see it. Every day, read the Bible verse for that day. When you read the Bible, you will find out how to obey God. He wants you to love reading His words in the Bible.

BIBLE READING PLAN

Sunday	*But his delight is in the law of the Lord and on his law he meditates day and night.* – Psalm 1:2
Monday	*I have hidden your word in my heart that I might not sin against you.* – Psalm 119:11
Tuesday	*Do not let this Book of the Law depart from your mouth; meditate on it day and night, so that you may be careful to do everything written in it. Then you will be prosperous and successful.* – Joshua 1:8
Wednesday	*Your word is a lamp to my feet and a light for my path.* – Psalm 119:105
Thursday	*Do not merely listen to the word and so deceive yourselves. Do what it says.* – James 1:22
Friday	*Children, obey your parents in the Lord, for this is right.* – Ephesians 6:1
Saturday	*My son, keep my words and store up my commandments within you.* – Proverbs 7:1

The Wise Men Worship Jesus the King

MATTHEW 2:1-12

✓MEMORY VERSE

Where is the one who has been born king of the Jews? We saw his star in the east and have come to worship him.
~ Matthew 2:2

WHAT YOU NEED

- page 66, duplicated
- blue construction paper
- glue

BEFORE CLASS

Duplicate a pattern page for each child. Make a sample craft to show the children.

WHAT TO DO

1. Introduce the lesson by explaining the meaning of the word "worship." Say, **Worship is showing honor and respect. It's showing God you believe He is God and you are willing to treat Him as the Ruler of your life.**
2. Tell the story from Matthew 2:1-12. Say, **The Wise Men had never heard of Jesus before. But they saw His special star and knew this star was an announcement that a very important King was about to be born. They wanted to come so they could worship King Jesus.**
3. Show the sample craft.
4. Distribute a pattern page to each child.
5. Say the memory verse.
6. Instruct students to cut out the stars and glue them on the construction paper in the correct word order according to the verse at the bottom of the page. Ask them to answer the question at the top of the page. Say, **We can worship King Jesus too.**

EXTRA TIME

Make a bulletin board, entitled "Ways To Worship King Jesus." Use the stars on the pattern page as a pattern to cut out stars out of card stock, and cover them with foil. Have the children use markers to write ways they can worship God on the stars. Suggest such ideas as pray, sing, obey, draw, give gifts, or praise.

Five Minute

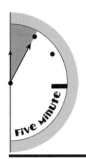

Place the stars in the right order according to the memory verse below. Why did the Wise Men come to see baby Jesus?

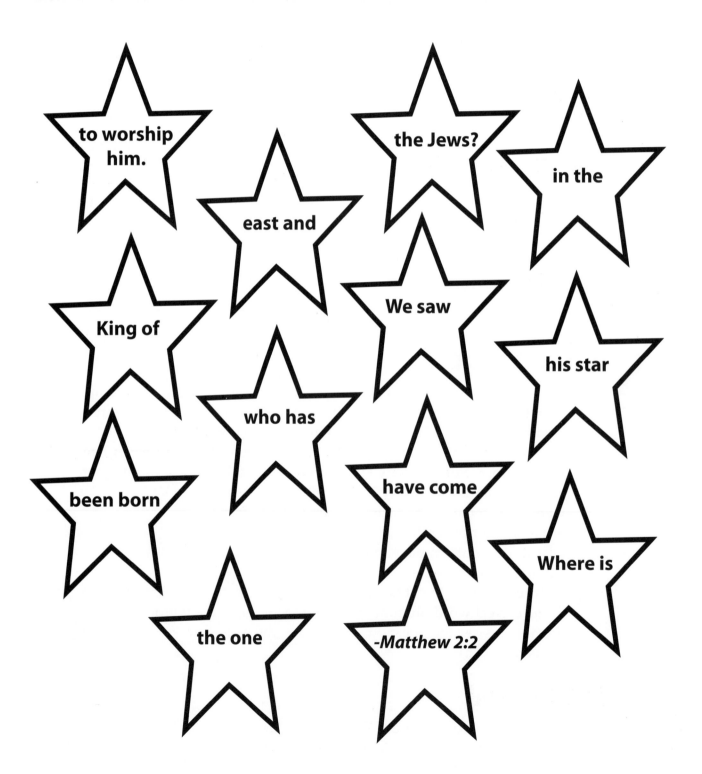

to worship him.

the Jews?

in the

east and

King of

We saw

his star

who has

been born

have come

Where is

the one

-Matthew 2:2

King Jesus Enters Jerusalem

MATTHEW 21:1-16

✓MEMORY VERSE

Hosanna! Blessed is he who comes in the name of the Lord! Blessed is the King of Israel!
~ John 12:13

WHAT YOU NEED

- page 68, duplicated
- pencils
- green crayons
- scissors

BEFORE CLASS

Duplicate a pattern page for each child. Make a sample craft to show the children.

WHAT TO DO

1. Introduce the lesson by asking, **What would you do if someone very important was coming to town and was going to walk down the main street of town?** Tell the story from Matthew 21:1-16. Say, **Many people, including children, were excited to see Jesus. They showed Jesus honor by waving branches of trees and shouting praise to God. Even though we can't see Jesus, we can also sing and shout praises to God in honor of King Jesus.**
2. Show the sample craft.
3. Distribute a pattern page to each child.
4. Say the memory verse.
5. Direct the children to write their own praise statements on the lines below the memory verse on the palm branch. Have children lightly color the palm branch green, then cut it out. As you have time, let the kids take turns waving their palm branches and shouting their praise poems.

EXTRA TIME

Reenact today's story by choosing someone to be Jesus. Have "Jesus" and the other children march around the room, waving their pattern page palm branches and shouting the memory verse and the praise poems they have written.

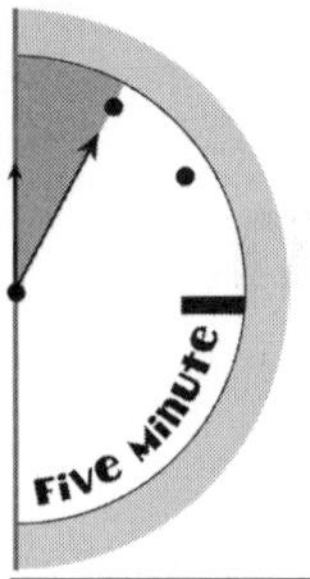

Write your own praise song. Cut out the palm leaf and shout your praise to King Jesus!

Hosanna!

Hosanna!

Hosanna! Blessed is he who comes in the name of the Lord!
Blessed is the King of Israel!
–John 12:13

God Rescues His People From Slavery

PSALM 105:1-5,23-38,43-45

✓MEMORY VERSE

He brought out his people with rejoicing,
his chosen ones with shouts of joy.
~ Psalm 105:43

WHAT YOU NEED

- page 70, duplicated on card stock
- assortment of coins

BEFORE CLASS

Duplicate a pattern page for every two to four children. If available, laminate the game boards using a laminating machine.

WHAT TO DO

1. Introduce the lesson by telling the story of how God rescued the Israelites from slavery in Egypt, using the summary found in Psalm 105:1-5, 23-38, 43-45. Refer to Exodus 7-12 to refresh your memory if you need to. Say, **Only God could cause these plagues to happen. God used the plagues to try to convince Pharaoh of His power. Only after his country was totally ruined did Pharaoh agree to let the Israelites leave Egypt.**
2. Make groups of two to four children. Distribute a pattern page to each group.
3. Read the memory verse together.
4. Have the groups play the game. Use pennies for game markers and a nickel for the game dice to determine movement on the game board: heads move forward one space, tails moves forward two spaces.
5. After everyone has finished playing, read the memory verse together. Ask, **How do you think the Israelites felt when they left Egypt? Do you think they understood why Pharaoh let them leave?** Say, **After seeing God's power, the Israelites were convinced it was God who rescued them from slavery.**

EXTRA TIME

Have the children read the story from Psalm 105:1-5, 23-30, 43-45 dramatically. Copy the Bible passage, dividing it into individual verses. Give each child a verse to read. Have them stand in a line and dramatically read the verses in order.

Five Minute

How did God get His people out of Egypt? Play this game with a friend to find out.

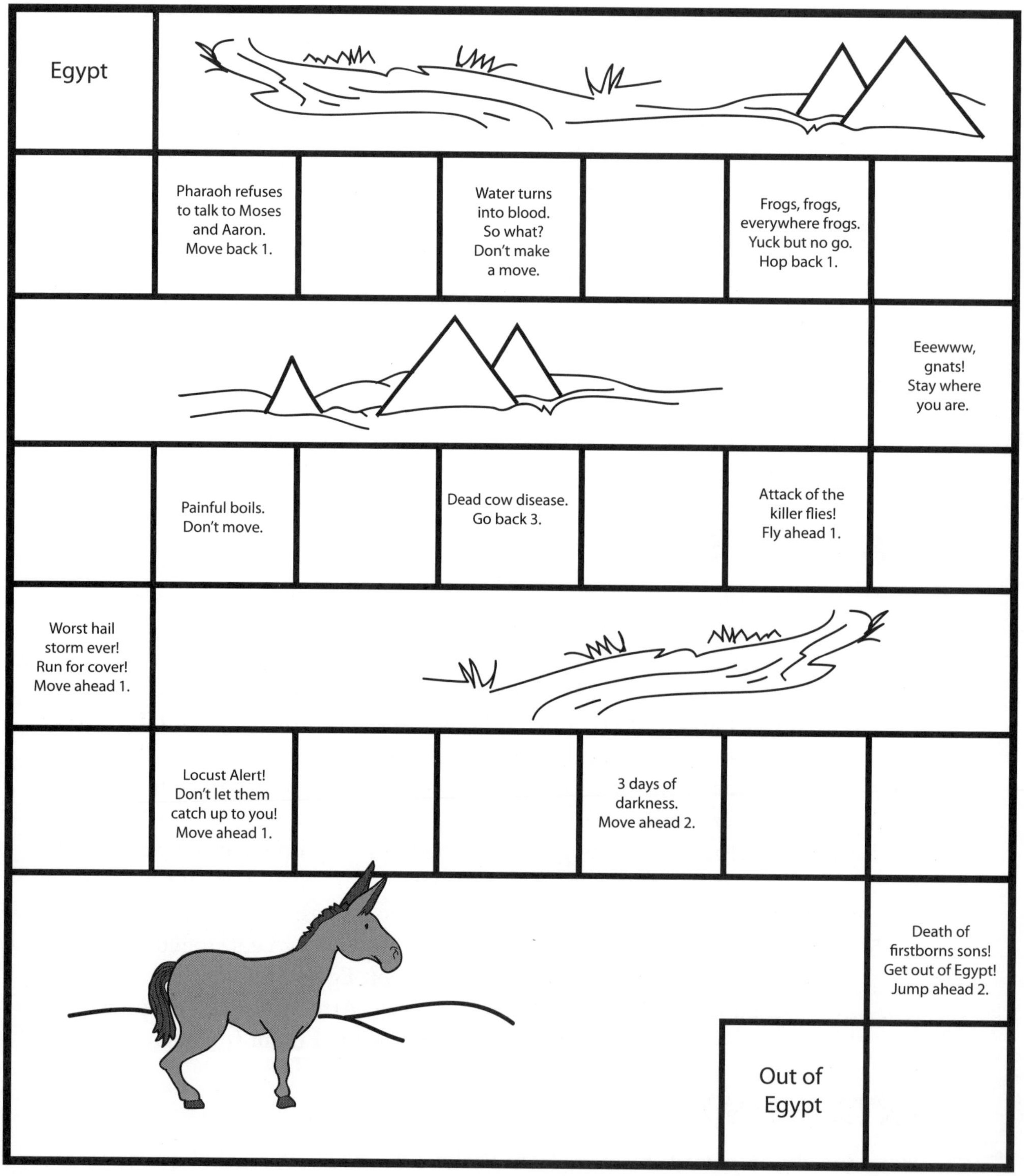
Egypt
Pharaoh refuses to talk to Moses and Aaron. Move back 1.
Water turns into blood. So what? Don't make a move.
Frogs, frogs, everywhere frogs. Yuck but no go. Hop back 1.
Eeewww, gnats! Stay where you are.
Attack of the killer flies! Fly ahead 1.
Dead cow disease. Go back 3.
Painful boils. Don't move.
Worst hail storm ever! Run for cover! Move ahead 1.
Locust Alert! Don't let them catch up to you! Move ahead 1.
3 days of darkness. Move ahead 2.
Death of firstborns sons! Get out of Egypt! Jump ahead 2.
Out of Egypt

He brought out his people with rejoicing, his chosen ones with shouts of joy.
– Psalm 105:43

God Helps Daniel Do the Right Thing

DANIEL 1

✓MEMORY VERSE

But Daniel resolved not to defile himself with the royal food and wine, and he asked the chief official for permission not to defile himself this way.
~ Daniel 1:8

WHAT YOU NEED

- page 72, duplicated
- pencils

BEFORE CLASS

Duplicate a pattern page for each child.

WHAT TO DO

1. Introduce the lesson by telling the story from Daniel 1. Say, **God gave the Israelites laws about what food they should and shouldn't eat. Other nations often ate food they had first sacrificed to idols (false gods). Daniel did not feel it was right for him to eat food offered to false gods or food that God said he shouldn't eat. Daniel believed God could keep him healthy even if he just ate vegetables.**
2. Distribute a pattern page to each child.
3. Say the memory verse.
4. Have kids unscramble the letters in the dinner menu to discover what Daniel asked to eat. Ask, **Are there times we need to make different choices than everyone around us because that's what God would want us to do?**

EXTRA TIME

Serve the children a variety of raw vegetables with a dip, and water to drink. Ask, **Do you think you could live on just vegetables?** Say, **Daniel did. God made Daniel more healthy than everyone else even though he was eating just vegetables.**

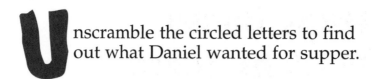

Unscramble the circled letters to find out what Daniel wanted for supper.

TONIGHT AT KING NEB'S TABLE

DINNER MENU

veal cutlets in cream sauce
glazed ham
frog legs
peas and carrots
cucumber salad
vanilla ice cream

Write the circled letters here: ___ ___ ___ ___ ___ ___ ___ ___ ___ ___

BEVERAGE LIST

wine
Goat's milk
tea
Grape soda
coffee

Write the circled letters here: ___ ___ ___ ___ ___

Daniel wanted ___ ___ ___ ___ ___ ___ ___ ___ ___ ___ **and**

___ ___ ___ ___ ___ **for dinner.**

But Daniel resolved not to defile himself with the royal food and wine and he asked the chief official for permission not to defile himself this way.
– Daniel 1:8

The solution is on page 96.

God Protects Daniel From the Lions

DANIEL 6

✓MEMORY VERSE

My God sent his angel, and he shut the mouths of the lions. They have not hurt me, because I was found innocent in his sight.
~ Daniel 6:22

WHAT YOU NEED

- page 74, duplicated
- crayons
- scissors
- lunch size paper bags
- glue sticks
- transparent tape

BEFORE CLASS

Duplicate a pattern page for each child. Make a sample craft to show the children.

WHAT TO DO

1. Introduce the lesson by telling the story from Daniel 6. Say, **God saved Daniel from the lions because Daniel kept praying to God even though it was against the law.**
2. Show the sample craft to the children.
3. Distribute a pattern page to each child.
4. Say the memory verse.
5. Have the children color the lion's face, then cut out the two parts and glue them on a paper bag to make a paper bag puppet. Have them tape the mouth shut then tape the memory verse over the mouth.
6. Have the children retell the story, using their puppets. Have them talk while keeping their mouths closed. Say, **God's power kept the lions' mouths closed so they wouldn't hurt Daniel.**

EXTRA TIME

Play a game of freeze tag. Establish a start and finish line. Choose two or three children to stand in the middle as the "lions." Everyone else will run from one line to the other. If a "lion" tags a player, the player must "freeze." Another player can unfreeze them so they can continue to run to the other side. Say, **God kept the lions from touching Daniel so he stayed safe even though he couldn't get away from them.**

Make a lion puppet to tell the story about Daniel in the lion pit.

My God sent his angel, and he shut the mouths of the lions.
They have not hurt me because I was found innocent in his sight.
– Daniel 6:22

Nehemiah Helps His People

NEHEMIAH 1, 2:1-9

Five Minute

✓MEMORY VERSE

Oh Lord, let your ear be attentive to the prayer of this your servant and to the prayers of your servants who delight in revering your name.
~ Nehemiah 1:11

WHAT YOU NEED

- page 76, duplicated
- scissors
- transparent tape
- markers
- crayons

BEFORE CLASS

Duplicate a pattern page for each child. Make a sample craft to show the children but do not draw anything in the blank panels.

WHAT TO DO

1. Introduce the lesson by telling the story from Nehemiah 1, 2:1-9. Ask, **What did Nehemiah do when he heard about the broken walls and burned gates of Jerusalem? What did he do when the king asked him what was wrong?**
2. Show the sample craft to the children.
3. Distribute a pattern page to each child. Say the memory verse.
4. Have children cut apart the panels on the pattern page and tape them together in one long strip. Discuss the first panel. Ask, **What did Nehemiah do when he heard the news about Jerusalem?** Ask the children to draw a picture of Nehemiah praying. Point to the third panel. Ask, **What did Nehemiah do next?** Have the children draw a picture of Nehemiah silently praying while standing before the king. Allow students to color the story strip.

EXTRA TIME

Have students turn their story strips over and draw a picture of a problem they or a group of children might face such as needing to talk to a school principal about the school helping a local needy family. Have them draw a picture of themselves praying about the problem. The third picture could show how God might answer their prayer. Say, **Whenever you have to talk to someone about a problem, you can pray first and God will help you do the thing that is hard to do.**

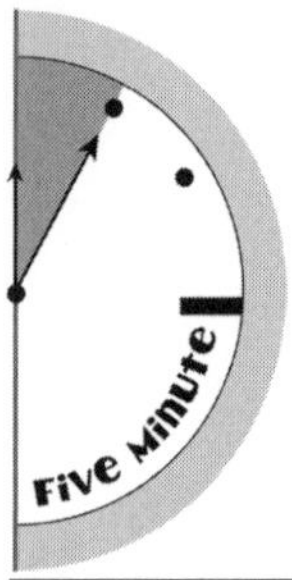

Make a story strip. In the blank squares, draw in the missing scenes from the story.

Oh Lord, let your ear be attentive to the prayer of this your servant and to the prayers of your servants who delight in revering your name.
– Nehemiah 1:11

The Shepherds Hear About Jesus

LUKE 2:1-20

✓MEMORY VERSE

Today in the town of David a Savior has been born to you; he is Christ the Lord.
~ Luke 2:11

WHAT YOU NEED

- page 78, duplicated
- pencils
- markers
- stickers

BEFORE CLASS

Duplicate a pattern page for each child. Make a sample craft to show the children.

WHAT TO DO

1. Introduce the lesson by telling the story from Luke 2:1-20. Ask, **Why did the angel call the baby a Savior?** Say, **For many years, God had promised to send a Savior called the Messiah. The angel told the shepherds that the baby born in Bethlehem was God's promised Messiah.**
2. Show the sample craft to the children.
3. Distribute a pattern page to each child.
4. Say the memory verse. Have the children repeat the verse with you.
5. Show the children how to fold the card in quarters. Have them fill in the information on the inside of the card, then decorate the card with markers and appropriate stickers. Say, **When a baby is born, the family sends out birth announcements. After the shepherds saw the baby Jesus, they told everyone they met the good news. You can give your birth announcement to someone to tell them the good news about Jesus.**

EXTRA TIME

Play the game, "Telephone." Seat the children in a line. Whisper, "A Savior is born." in the ear of the first child. That child will whisper the message to the next person, who will in turn whisper it to the next person. The last child stands and says what he thinks the message is. Repeat the game with, "He is Christ the Lord."

Five Minute

Cut out the card and fold on the dotted lines. Fill in the blanks and draw pictures to tell about the birth of baby Jesus.

Today in the town
of David a Savior
has been born to you;
he is Christ the Lord.
-Luke 2:11

Birth Announcement:

A _______ *Is Born!*

fold →

Who: ____________________

When: ____________________

Where: ____________________

fold →

The Boy Jesus in the Temple

LUKE 2:41-52

✓MEMORY VERSE

And Jesus grew in wisdom and stature,
and in favor with God and men.
~ Luke 2:52

WHAT YOU NEED

- page 80, duplicated on card stock
- pennies

BEFORE CLASS

Duplicate a pattern page for every three to four children.

WHAT TO DO

1. Introduce the lesson by telling the story from Luke 2:41-52. Say, **To do the work God had planned for Him, Jesus needed to grow up and become strong in every way. His body and His mind grew. He grew in how He got along with other people and also with God. God wants us to grow up in the same four ways.**
2. Divide the group into smaller groups of three to four children. Give each group a pattern page.
3. Say the memory verse. Make the connection between the labels on the shield and the words in the memory verse: Body = stature; Mind = wisdom, Friends = in favor with man; and Faith in God = in favor with God.
4. Explain how to play the game. Children take turns placing the penny on the page number below the memory verse and flicking it into one of the four sections of the shield. They will select one of the options and answer it or do it before passing the penny to the next person. Say, **See? You are growing in every way—just like Jesus!**

EXTRA TIME

Teach your children the memory verse to the tune of "Row, Row, Row Your Boat," using these lyrics, "Jesus grew and grew/According to God's plan/Wisdom, stature, in favor too/Wi-ith God and man." Ask the children to name ways they are growing in each of the four ways.

Play this game with your friends. Place a penny on the memory verse. Shoot it with your index finger. Answer a question in the section where it lands.

BODY:

- Do three jumping jacks.
- Tie your shoes.
- Show your arm muscles.

MIND:

- What is 2 + 2?
- Sing your favorite song.
- Tell how to make a peanut butter and jelly sandwich.

FRIENDS:

- Give a hug to the person next to you.
- Tell how to act if a stranger walked into the room.
- Tell the person next to you something you like about them.

FAITH IN GOD:

- Repeat your favorite Bible verse.
- When you have a problem, what would God like you to do?
- Why did Jesus die on the cross?
- Where do Christians go when they die?

And Jesus grew in wisdom and stature, and in favor with God and men.
– Luke 2:52

Jesus' Power Over a Storm

MATTHEW 8:23-27

✓MEMORY VERSE

You rule over the surging sea; when its waves mount up, you still them.
~ Psalm 89:9

WHAT YOU NEED

- page 82, duplicated
- pencils
- colored pencils or markers

BEFORE CLASS

Duplicate a pattern page for each child.

WHAT TO DO

1. Introduce the lesson by telling the story from Matthew 8:23-27. Ask, **How bad was the storm? How afraid were the disciples? How quickly did the storm go away? Have you ever been afraid in a bad storm? What can you do when you are afraid?**
2. Distribute a pattern page to each child.
3. Say the memory verse.
4. Tell the children to write the phrase, "Lord, save us" on each blank line. Read the poem as a responsive reading. Ask a volunteer to read the printed words and everyone else to respond by saying, "Lord, save us." Let the children draw storm pictures around the border such as raindrops and lightening bolts. Say**, Jesus can rescue us from anything. As God's Son, He has the power to save us.**

EXTRA TIME

Fill a two-liter plastic bottle half full of water. Put the lid on and turn it on its side. Slosh the water vigorously, then lay the bottle on a table. Ask, **How long does it take for the water to stop moving?** Let students watch a clock to see. Say, **When Jesus ordered the storm to stop, the waves on the lake settled down immediately. Jesus could do this because He is God's Son.**

Five Minute

Write, "Lord, save us" on the blank lines.
Decorate your poem page with storm pictures.
Read your poem to a friend.

Tornadoes and thunderstorms

____

Hurricanes and blizzards

____

No matter what the storm

____

All you need to say is

____

And Jesus will be there.

He is with you all the time!

You rule over the surging sea; when its waves mount up, you still them.
– Psalm 89:9

Five Minute

Jesus Meets a Woman at a Well

JOHN 4:4-42

✓ MEMORY VERSE

We know that this man really is the Savior of the world.
~ John 4:42

WHAT YOU NEED

- page 83, duplicated
- pencils

BEFORE CLASS

Duplicate a pattern page for each child. Complete a sample story to show the children.

WHAT TO DO

1. Introduce the lesson by telling the story from John 4:4-42. Say, **Jesus offered the woman living water. He meant He could give her life forever because He was God's Son. He wanted her to believe He was the Savior of the world.**
2. Show the sample story to the children.
3. Distribute a pattern page to each child.
4. Say the memory verse.
5. Have students complete the story by filling in the blanks with the letter "W." When everyone has finished the story, select volunteers to play the parts of a narrator, Jesus, and the woman. Everyone else can be the townspeople. Read through the story together. Say, **The woman learned that true worship of God is to believe that Jesus is the Savior of the world.**

EXTRA TIME

Have students turn their pages over and draw a picture of a way they can worship God. Say, **The best way to worship is to tell God you believe Jesus is the Savior of the world and you believe Jesus has the power to let you live forever with Him.**

W is for Worship! Fill in the blanks with the letter W to complete the story.

Narrator: Jesus ____anted ____ater from a ____ell. He asked a ____oman for __ater from the ____ell.

_____**oman:** ____hy are you asking me for ____ater?"

Jesus: If you knew ____ho I ____as you ____ould ask me for ____ater. I ____ill give you living ____ater."

Narrator: The ____oman ____hined . . .

_____**oman:** I ____ant living ____ater. But ____hy do your people say to ____orship God in Jerusalem? ____e ____orship God on a mountain.

Jesus: God ____ants you to ____orship in spirit and in truth.

_____**oman:** ____hen the Savior of the ____orld comes, he ____ill help us understand everything.

Jesus: I ____ho speak to you am He.

Narrator: The ____oman left her ____ater jar at the ____ell and ran back to town. She told everyone:

_____**oman:** Come meet a man ____ho told me everything I ever did. Could this be the Savior?

Narrator: ____hen the people met Jesus, they said to the ____oman at the ____ell:

Townspeople: ____e no longer believe just because of ____hat you said; now ____e have heard for ourselves and ____e know that this man really is the Savior of the ____orld."

We know that this man really is the Savior of the world.
–John 4:42

Zaccheus Meets Jesus

LUKE 19:1-10

✓MEMORY VERSE

Jesus said to him, "Today salvation has come to this house."
~ Luke 19:9

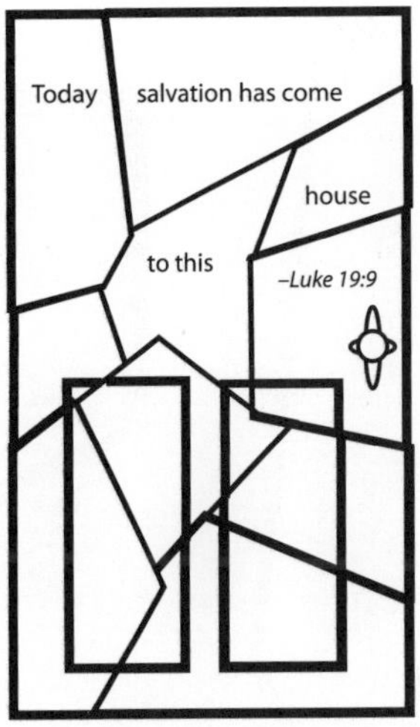

Today
salvation has come
house
to this
–Luke 19:9

WHAT YOU NEED

- page 86, duplicated
- scissors
- card stock
- glue

BEFORE CLASS

Duplicate a pattern page for each child. Make a sample craft to show the children. Mount your puzzle on a piece of card stock.

WHAT TO DO

1. Introduce the lesson by telling the story from Luke 19:1-10. Say, **Zaccheus' job was to collect taxes. Often tax collectors were dishonest people.** Ask, **What did Zaccheus do so he could see Jesus? What promise did Zaccheus make to Jesus?**
2. Show a sample craft to the children. Read the memory verse together.
3. Distribute a pattern page to each child.
4. Have the children cut out the puzzle pieces and put the puzzle together. As children complete the puzzle, have them read the memory verse to you. Say, **Zaccheus promised Jesus he would change. He would give half his money to the poor and if he had cheated anyone, he would make it up to them. That's why Jesus said, "Salvation has come to this house." If we want Jesus to save us so we can live forever with Him, we have to be willing to change what we do and start following Him.**

EXTRA TIME

Have students disassemble their puzzles. On the other side of the puzzle pieces, have them write a promise to God of a way they will change their behavior so they are following Jesus. Have them write the promise as one or two words per piece, so that the words are in order when the puzzle is assembled. Have them turn over the pieces and glue to a piece of card stock, memory verse side up. Say, **Now only God and you know the promise you have made to Him.**

Cut out the puzzle and put it together to find out what Jesus said to Zaccheus.

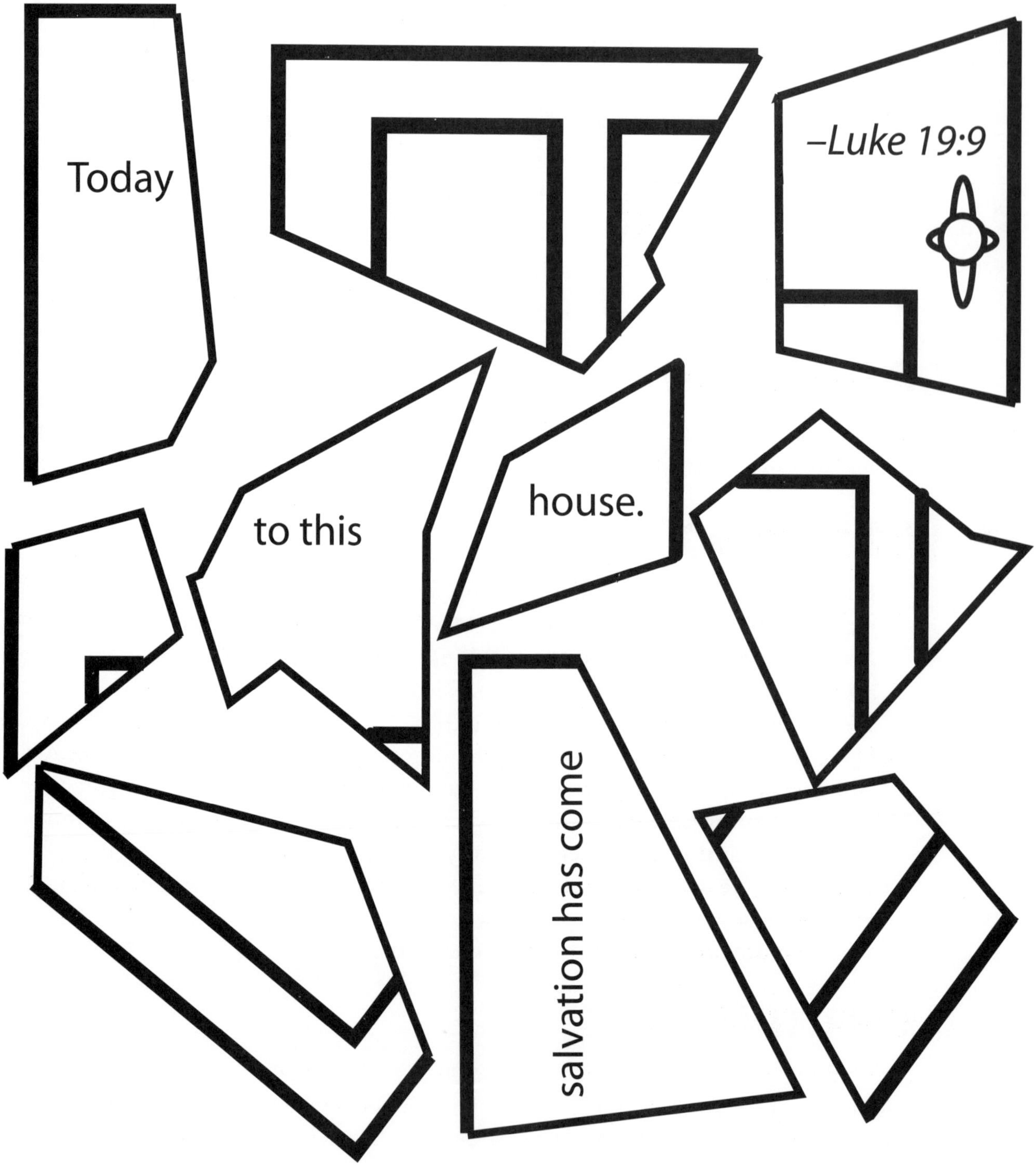
Today
to this
house.
salvation has come
–Luke 19:9

The solution is on page 96.

Jesus Brings Lazarus Back to Life

JOHN 11

✓MEMORY VERSE

I am the resurrection and the life. He who believes in me will live, even though he dies.
~ John 11:25

WHAT YOU NEED

- page 88, duplicated
- scissors
- hole punch
- ribbon
- crayons or markers
- transparent tape

BEFORE CLASS

Duplicate a pattern page for each child. Make a sample craft to show the children.

WHAT TO DO

1. Introduce the lesson by telling the story from John 11. Say, **Before Jesus brought Lazarus back to life, he had a talk with Martha, Lazarus' sister.** Ask an older reader to read John 11:17-27. Say, **Martha believed her brother would live again when the world comes to an end. Jesus tried to tell her that He had the power to make her brother live again right then. Why could Jesus do this?**
2. Show the sample craft to the children.
3. Distribute a pattern page to each child.
4. Read the memory verse.
5. Have the children cut out the round bookmark, fold it in half, tape it together, punch a hole at the top, and string a ribbon through the hole. As time allows, let them color the picture. Ask, **If Jesus has the power to bring people back to life, do we need to be afraid of dying? If Jesus has the power to bring people back to life, what else would He have the power to do?** Encourage children to put the bookmark in their Bibles or other book at home.

EXTRA TIME

Use toilet paper to wrap a volunteer from head to toe. Explain that in Jesus' country, dead people were wrapped in grave cloths before they were buried. When Lazarus walked out of the tomb, Jesus told the sisters to unloose him. Have your "Lazarus" pretend to come back to life and break out of the grave clothes.

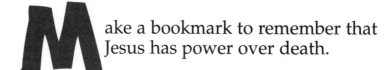

Make a bookmark to remember that Jesus has power over death.

I am the resurrection
and the life. He who
believes in me
will live, even
though he dies.
– John 11:25

Jesus Dies for Us

LUKE 22:47-23:56

✓MEMORY VERSE

For God so loved the world that he gave his one and only Son, that whoever believes in him shall not perish but have eternal life.
~ John 3:16

WHAT YOU NEED

- page 90, duplicated
- string
- red tempera paint
- newspaper
- foil pie plates
- water for cleanup

BEFORE CLASS

Duplicate a pattern page for each child. Make a sample craft to show the children. Cut the string in 1 ½, 6, and 8-inch lengths.

WHAT TO DO

1. Introduce the lesson by telling the story from Luke 22:47-23:56. Ask the children review questions about the story. Say, **Jesus could have stopped those evil men from killing Him. He chose to die because He wanted to save us from the punishment we deserve for the wrong we've done. He wanted to take the punishment for us.**
2. Show the sample craft to the children.
3. Distribute a pattern page and a string of each length to each child. Say the memory verse together.
4. Have the children fold their page in half then unfold it. Spread newspaper over the work area. Put paint in several foil plates. Have children take one string at a time, dip it in the paint, squeeze out the extra paint, and lay it carefully on the line that it fits. They will fold the paper over, pressing carefully and evenly on the strings, then unfold the paper and remove the strings. Say, **Jesus died on the cross because He loves you and wants you to live forever with Him after you die.**

EXTRA TIME

Sing the following words to the tune of "Mary Had A Little Lamb:" "Jesus came and died for me, died for me, died for me/Jesus came and died for me/So that I may live." Sing other praise songs that tell about Jesus' gift of salvation.

Crease your paper in half. Dip string in red paint and lay along the lines. Fold your paper over, unfold it and remove the strings. See why Jesus loves you?

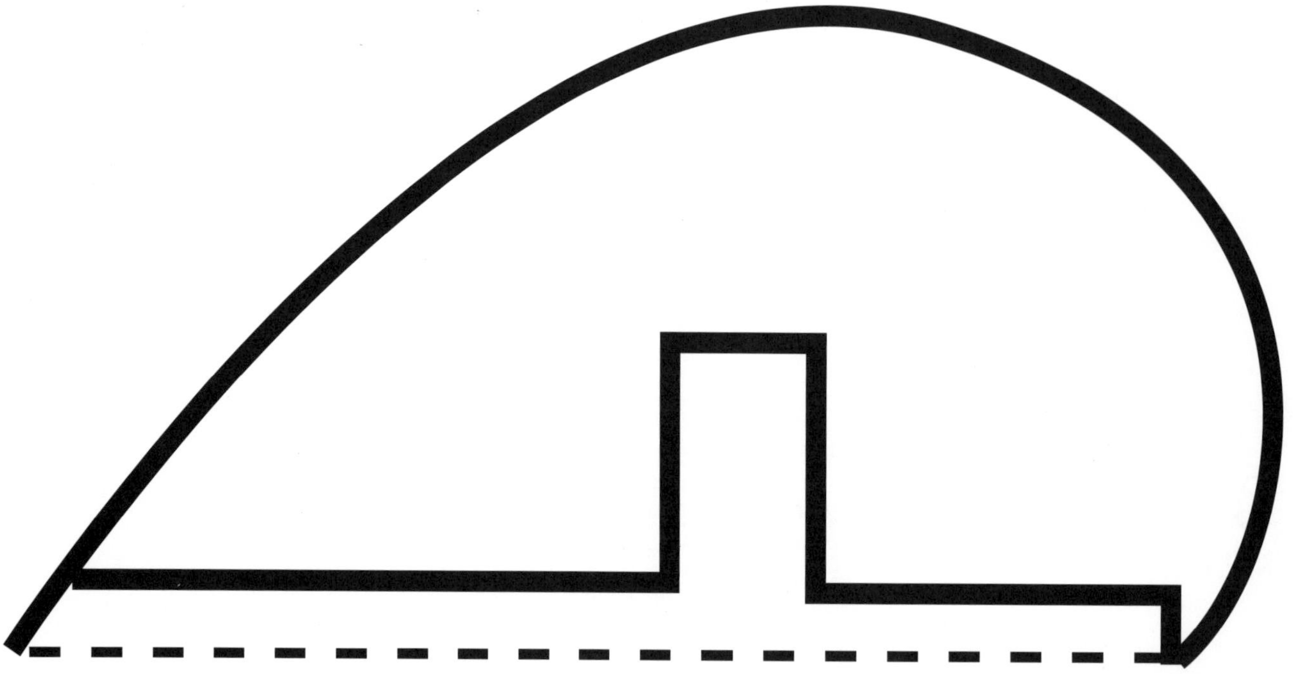

For God so loved the world that he gave his one and only Son, that whoever believes in him shall not perish but have eternal life.
– John 3:16

Jesus Comes Back to Life

LUKE 24:1-12

✓MEMORY VERSE

He is not here; he has risen!
~ Luke 24:6

WHAT YOU NEED

- page 92, duplicated
- crayons

BEFORE CLASS

Duplicate a pattern page for each child.

WHAT TO DO

1. Introduce the lesson by telling the story from Luke 24:1-12. Ask, **Is it possible for someone to come back to life after they have died? What happened to Jesus' body? How could Jesus come back to life?**
2. Distribute a pattern page to each child.
3. Say the memory verse.
4. Tell children to color the sections of the page that have a dot, using the same color of crayon. After they have discovered the words, "He has risen," they may color the rest of the page using other colors. Say, **Because Jesus has the power to come back to life, He also has the power to let us live forever with Him after we die. Isn't that exciting news?**

EXTRA TIME

Write Christian messages or symbols on hard boiled eggs using a white crayon, such as, "Jesus Lives!", "He Rose", "He's Alive", or a picture of a cross and a tomb. Have the kids dye the eggs.

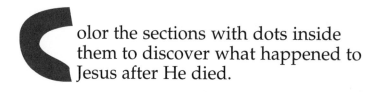

Color the sections with dots inside them to discover what happened to Jesus after He died.

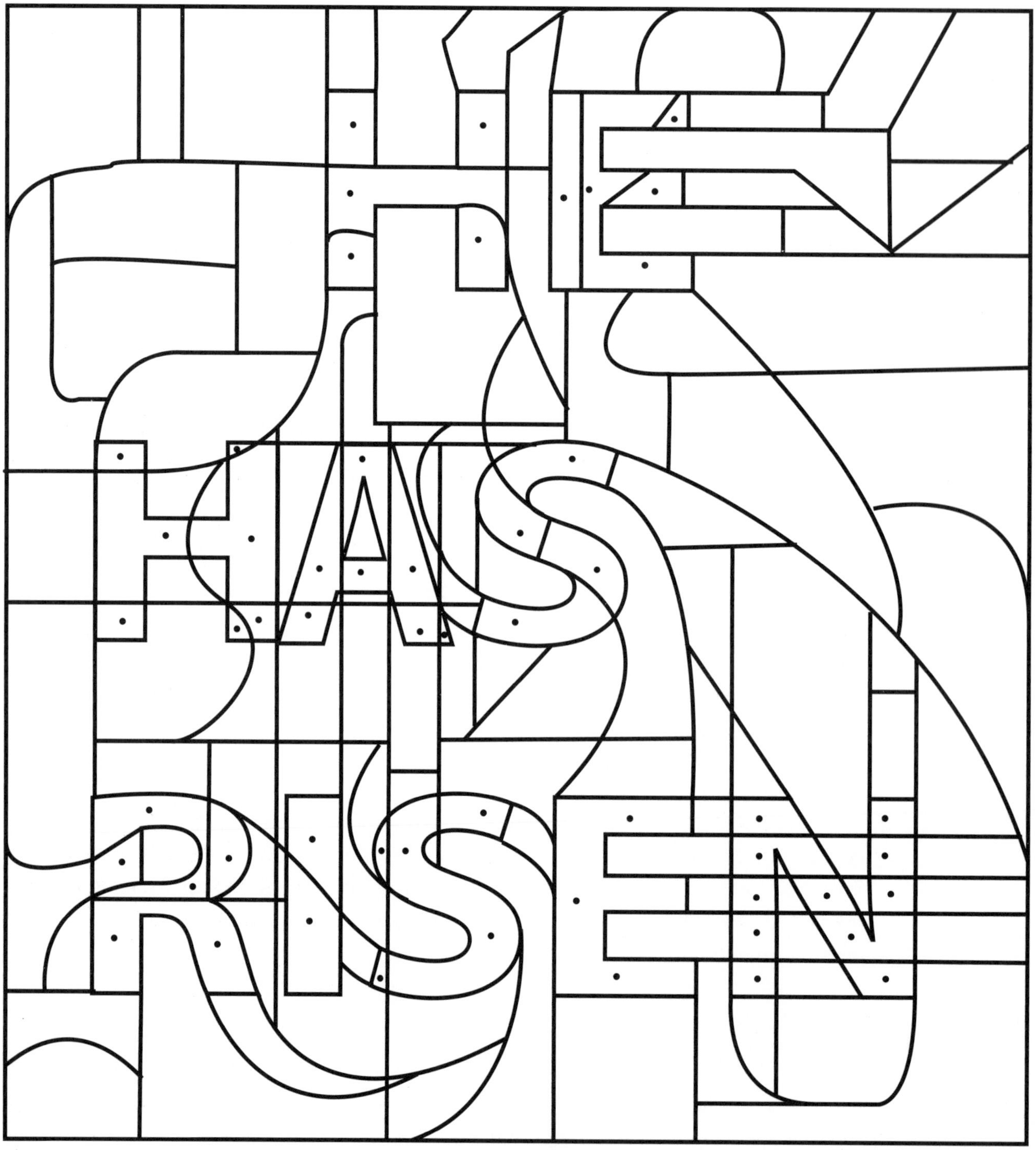

He is not here; he has risen!
– Luke 24:6

The solution is on page 96.

John Sees Heaven

REVELATIONS 20:11-15, 21:1-8

✓MEMORY VERSE

Then I saw a new heaven and a new earth; for the first heaven and the first earth had passed away, and there was no longer any sea.
~ Revelation 21:1

WHAT YOU NEED

- page 93, duplicated
- markers, crayons or colored pencils

BEFORE CLASS

Duplicate a pattern page for each child.

WHAT TO DO

1. Introduce the lesson by saying, **One day, a man named John got to see what Heaven will be like. He described it this way.** Read Revelation 20:11-15, 21:1-8. Ask, **According to what we just read, what will Heaven be like? Do you think you will like to live in a beautiful place where there is no pain and no sadness?**
2. Distribute a pattern page to each child.
3. Say the memory verse.
4. Ask the children to draw a picture of what they would like to do when they see Jesus in Heaven. Say, **It's hard to imagine living in a beautiful place forever. But that's what it will be like. Heaven will be better than anything we can imagine. And we'll be there because Jesus made it possible for us to be there. Isn't He wonderful?**

EXTRA TIME

Play a rhythm game. Seat the children in a circle. Have them slap their thighs twice, then clap twice while saying, "When I get to Heaven, I'm gonna..." As they pause, the children will take turns saying what they will do in heaven.

What will you do when you see Jesus in Heaven?

Will you worship Him?

Will you say "Hi" to Him?

Will you sing a song of praise?

Draw a picture of you and Jesus when you meet Him in Heaven.

Then I saw a new heaven and a new earth; for the first heaven and the first earth had passed away, and there was no longer any sea.
– Revelation 21:1

Puzzle Answers

Page 12

1. You shall have no other **gods** before me.
2. You shall not have any **idols**.
3. You shall not misuse the **name** of the Lord your God.
4. Remember the **Sabbath** day by keeping it holy.
5. **Honor** your father and mother.
6. You shall not **murder**.
7. You shall not **commit** adultery.
8. You shall not **steal**.
9. You shall not give **false** testimony.
10. You shall not **covet**.

Page 16

COURAGE

Page 24

I was hungry and you **GAVE ME SOMETHING TO EAT** (C)

I was thirsty and you **GAVE ME SOMETHING TO DRINK** (B)

I was a stranger and you **INVITED ME IN** (A)

I needed clothes and you **CLOTHED ME** (D)

I was sick and you **LOOKED AFTER ME** (F)

I was in prison and you **CAME TO VISIT ME** (E)

Page 26

All the crowns should be colored.

Page 28

Page 30

Two types of animals Saul didn't destroy: (sheep, cattle)

Two things Saul didn't do that he was supposed to do: (wait, destroy everything)

Who told Saul to fight: (Samuel)

*Walk in **all the ways** I command you that it may go well with you.*
– Jeremiah 7:23

Page 34

Tell them they did a good job.

Pray for them.

Tell someone else what a good job they did.

Work harder to do my best.

Page 36

Page 38

S	U	R	E	J	W	X	V	L	P
W	L	P	N	M	V	Z	S	G	J
R	E	K	X	R	J	K	Y	O	P
O	R	I	Z	E	D	S	G	H	K
N	Q	N	O	A	F	C	U	K	L
G	E	D	C	T	R	T	Y	H	J
P	T	E	A	C	H	F	G	K	T
X	V	Z	N	O	T	H	E	R	O
E	L	S	E	S	N	A	I	T	H

*Make **sure** that nobody pays back **wrong** for wrong, but always try to be **kind** to **each other**, and to everyone **else**.*
– 1 Thessalonians 5:15

Page 46

Page 48
needs

Page 50
The angel of the Lord encamps around those who fear Him, and He delivers them.
– Psalm 34:7

Page 72
Daniel wanted **vegetables** and **water** for dinner.

Page 86
Today, salvation has come to this house.
– Luke 19:9

Page 92
He Has Risen